Critical Issues in Library Personnel Management

RICHARD RUBIN

Editor

University of Illinois
Graduate School of Library and Information Science
Urbana-Champaign, Illinois

ALLERTON PARK INSTITUTE

Number 29

Papers Presented at the Allerton Park Institute

Sponsored by

University of Illinois
Graduate School of Library and Information Science

held

November 6-8, 1987
Allerton Conference Center
Robert Allerton Park
Monticello, Illinois

This Allerton Park Institute has also been published
as the Summer 1989 issue of *Library Trends*
(Volume 38, No. 1)

CONTENTS

Introduction

People run libraries; they provide the essential services, process the materials, prepare the budgets, and establish the policies and practices that shape the institution. This is not always recognized by a public that often perceives the library as a place for collections of books. Certainly, an important aspect of any library is an array of objects that contribute to library service: the media, physical facilities, and electronic technologies. But a human being is responsible for combining these elements into effective library service, and failures in library service are often failures to deal appropriately with human issues. Perhaps someday the wholly electronic library will make people unnecessary. But today the proliferation of library technologies has highlighted rather than diminished the vital role that people play in the changing library environment. The purpose of the 29th Allerton Conference was to identify and discuss some of these issues, and to provide a forum for exchange of ideas on critical issues in personnel management.

Managing personnel is an especially difficult task because the reasons people act as they do are varied and often opaque. The library manager, whose training emphasizes librarianship more than management, is forced to operate in this difficult environment with few guidelines. What motivates staff members? Martin Maehr, from the University of Illinois, addresses this issue in the general context of worker motivation. Similarly, Charles Martell explores the necessary conditions for high achievement in the library workplace. In each of these articles, the emphasis is on library workers as people. The articles are a recognition of the importance of human needs and the implicit potential of greater productivity in their fulfillment.

1

As the library environment becomes more and more complex, greater demands for flexibility are placed on a library manager and staff. Confronting this problem, Shay Baker offers some fruitful observations on managing resistance to change. Failure to deal with the human aspects of the workplace can have serious and negative consequences; one of these consequences is stress. Charles Bunge, professor of Library and Information Science, explores the role of stress in the workplace.

Although understanding the psychosocial aspects of a library worker is vital, the mechanics of personnel management also constitute a major concern for library managers. Kathleen Heim explores the topic of entry-level recruitment of employees in libraries based on the complex labor pool. It has become clear in today's litigious labor climate that what you do may be less important than how you do it. To this end, Anne Lipow examines the subject of training library staff. It is also necessary to deal effectively with the employee who has decided to leave for one reason or another. James Neal reviews key considerations in conducting the exit interview.

Organizational issues involving personnel must also be explored. Without doubt, collective bargaining has become a prominent issue in the minds of many managers. Norman Holman offers a perspective on bargaining in a public library. Of equal importance are issues concerning wage and salary administration. In an era of "comparable worth," the manner in which we value our jobs and compensate our employees is subject to considerable scrutiny and legal liability. Frederick Duda reviews some of the major points for academic librarians, while Christopher Bowen reviews a technique for wage and salary setting in a public library. The subject of job evaluation naturally leads to the subject of evaluating people in their jobs—performance evaluation. In this regard, Lucy Cohen offers suggestions for creating and conducting performance reviews.

Given the number of issues explored at the 29th Allerton Conference, obtaining perspective on many of the challenges of personnel is difficult. In a synthesis and summary of the Conference, Peggy Sullivan offers some guidance through a maze of issues that confront a personnel manager. Attempting to deal with the myriad issues of personnel management in one place, at one time, is, of course, doomed to superficiality in regard to any one topic. But this discourse is essential if managers are to confront, control, and deal with a fundamental force in libraries—the human being.

MARTIN L. MAEHR

Professor of Education and Psychology
University of Michigan
Ann Arbor, Michigan

Building Job Commitment Among Employees

ABSTRACT

This article is concerned with how persons in leadership roles can elicit the motivation, commitment, and personal investment of members of an organization. Recent research on employee motivation is briefly summarized and interpreted. It is argued that those in leadership roles bear a special responsibility for creating a sense of purpose in the organization. It is as leaders engage the members of an organization in establishing goals, in focusing on the purpose of their work and the mission of the organization, that they are most likely to elicit personal investment. The design and use of other management tasks, especially evaluation, play an important complementary role in reinforcing the sense of a shared purpose and therewith can contribute significantly to the development of employee commitment.

INTRODUCTION

One would have to be a 1980s Rip Van Winkle not to realize that "organizational effectiveness" has become a major, sometimes all consuming, problem. It is virtually impossible to pick up a newspaper or magazine without seeing a reference to this problem. Almost everyone who walks to a speaker's platform these days seems obliged to issue a call for reform of this or that practice or this or that organization—its effectiveness, efficiency, and productivity. The resounding theme through all this seems to be that if our society is to remain viable, if our way of life is to be retained, we must be more productive; the various organizations associated with such productivity must become more effective.

3

Perhaps it was initially our loss of a competitive edge to the Japanese—first in autos, later in TVs and stereos, and most recently in the basics of computer technology—that started this train of thought regarding productivity. But it soon turned to the effectiveness of public schools and then to our colleges and universities. It has, to date, touched virtually each and every organization and agency of significance. Consider, for example, that health care organizations are virtually under siege, even though they are hardly in competition with Japan.

And what about libraries? It is suspected that libraries and librarians have felt the same kind of effectiveness pressures that most organizations today are experiencing; it is virtually inevitable. The dollars are fewer; we are expected to do more with less.

Productivity has been one of the dominating issues of the day. Doubtless the recent volatility of the financial markets will reinforce what has already been a persistent and dominating concern. It is doubtful that these issues are just another fad. If anything they will likely increase in importance. Those concerned with issues of management cannot escape the scrutiny, the challenge—and perhaps also the opportunity—that this brings to their job.

THE IMPORTANCE OF WORKER/EMPLOYEE COMMITMENT

Organizational effectiveness—what it is and how you get it—is a complex issue. Simply defined, organizational effectiveness means accomplishing the goals of the organization. Implicitly or explicitly it often means accomplishing goals with a minimum of resources and doing it efficiently. To do that, one has to be careful how the resources available to an organization are managed and utilized. It means careful attention to such things as copying expenditures and to duplication of services and purchases, but it means much more than that.

Several weeks ago, Lester Thurow, a prominent economist and dean of the Sloan School of Management of M.I.T., presented the David Kinley lecture at the University of Illinois. In that lecture he alluded to a fact that he has regularly mentioned in the last several years: In order to have what we think we want to have in this society, a qualified work force is an absolute necessity; there has to be not only skillful, but also motivated and committed workers. Undoubtedly he would not object to his point being rephrased by saying that an effective society needs effective organizations and effective organizations exist only as there are committed workers. Employee commitment at all levels in the organization is the sine qua non of any effective organization. People have to be willing to give at least a day's work for a day's pay. They must be willing at times to adjust their needs to the needs of the organization—i.e., adjust their personal schedule as the job demands, pitch in to help out even when their job definition does not specify it.

Effective organizations this author has known and studied could not be effective if there weren't individuals in that organization—a significant number—who were fiercely loyal to it, a significant number who were commited to doing the jobs that needed to be done, a significant number who were willing to stick with the organization in good and bad times, a significant number who believed in the organization's ultimate worth.

In discussing employee commitment, the term *personal investment* comes to mind since it seems to suggest the kind of personal involvement needed in an effective organization. And essentially two things are meant by that term (for a fuller discussion see Maehr and Braskamp, 1986). First, the term implies a certain personal identification which involves loyalty—staying with the organization through thick and thin. Second, the term implies a willingness to put forth one's best efforts in making the organization work.

All have the capacity to be committed to something. All have talent and energy to commit. The question is how will they choose to invest these personal resources that they possess? Why do persons commit their time and talent in this case but not in that one? The inevitable question of concern is What is there about a particular job or job context that does not serve to elicit worker investment? There is not really anything "wrong" with the person—he or she is not lacking in drive; he or she is not lazy. She or he simply is not attracted to the task in this case.

WHAT CONDITIONS ENCOURAGE COMMITMENT?

It is doubtful whether any of you would be here if you did not essentially agree with most of what has been said thus far—i.e., organizational effectiveness is important; organizational effectiveness is significantly dependent on employee commitment. In a way, this is "preaching to the choir." The significant question is What conditions are likely to encourage such commitment?

Over the years change occurs in the variety of strategies initiating motivation because encouraging personal investment and employee commitment have been discussed, developed, and implemented. Reviewing what has been said in this regard one might suggest that in general there are thought to be three "pressure points" for change: the person, the job, and the organization.

In the first case, one can view the problem as resting particularly in the individual and work on changing something about him or her. Or, if change is not easy, one can concentrate on selecting the "right" persons; that is, persons who are judged likely to exhibit high personal investment in the role assigned. In the main this has been the approach pursued by such notables in the area as David McClelland (1978, 1985; McClelland & Winter, 1971).

The second and third possible pressure points for change involve the situation. In this case the focus is not so much on the characteristics of individuals but on features of the situation that will bring about change. Within the broad category of "situation" one can specify two important subcategories. First, there is the *task*, the specific role to be played by the person; the job to be done. From the work of Hackman and Oldham (1980), as well as that of others, it is clear that there are a variety of factors that can be adjusted to change the task which will in turn affect motivation. Second, as will become increasingly evident in this address, the job situation, the task to be done, or the role to be played, is not the sole determining feature of the context. The nature, structure, policies, goals, and values of the organization as a whole make a difference.

The pragmatic question for those who are in roles where they must manage motivation is whether it is more practical to change the situation or to select the persons who happen to hold the desired meaning biases. If the latter is chosen, enhancing personal investment in an organization will involve especially a stress on recruitment, personnel selection, or perhaps an emphasis on changing persons to fit job and organizational expectations. If the former strategy is pursued, then the stress is on changing the work situation—redesigning the job, changing the work climate, or designing the organizational culture to enhance the personal investment of all regardless of the individual biases they may bring to the situation.

While each of these strategies may have a role to play in managing personal investment, the one that seems most practicable so far as leaders are concerned relates to changing the organizational context. Thus managers, administrators—i.e., leaders—cannot rely solely or primarily on personnel selection or placement as the means for influencing the commitment—i.e., the personal investment of their staff. They have too few opportunities to select and place. But there is some reason to believe that they can affect the context in which their staff works. In particular, there is some reason to believe that they can have their most important affects on staff commitment through the way they manage organizational climate and culture (Maehr, 1987).

And, within that broader domain, there is reason to believe that it is especially important to concentrate on setting goals, defining the purpose of the organization, and articulating a sense of direction. In short, it is as the leader establishes or articulates, and therewith communicates, a mission that staff are likely to exhibit personal investment.

A simple way of putting this is to suggest that the leader's role in eliciting motivation and commitment begins and ends with an attempt to make work meaningful. A major function in this regard is to convey the purposes of the organization—where it is going—and how the individual contributes to and is a part of this overall direction of the organization. How can the leader/manager/administrator create conditions which foster such sense of direction and which give meaning to the employee's efforts?

What the leader can do revolves significantly around three critical functions: diagnosis/assessment, goal and mission establishment, and evaluation/performance appraisal. While each of these processes is worthy of a detailed discussion in its own right, this discussion will be limited to a few brief words in each case. The reason for this is: first, the time is short; and second, there is an unwillingness to get so involved in describing the trees that we forget that the forest is "the thing." Strategies, tactics, and processes are important. These processes can be instrumental in establishing a sense of purpose in an organization. But in the final analysis they must be part of a broader whole. That broader whole is the overwhelming reason for making purpose important in the organization.

Diagnosis/Assessment

It is self evident that as a leader/manager/administrator you are not likely to create an organization from scratch with goals and purposes of only your choosing. One gets placed into an ongoing system and has to accept an organization or work group as it comes to you and perhaps inch it along to what you think it should be. Whether or not the overall culture of the organization, its goals, and sense of purpose need changing, one somehow needs to grasp what it is. That is what "diagnosis/assessment" is about.

If indeed the communication of a "mission" and the establishment of a certain organizational culture is important, then one does well to exercise concern by assessing just what that culture and mission are perceived to be. A diagnosis/assessment approach to the analysis of the character and operation of an organization and its units is desirable— and increasingly possible (see, for example, Braskamp & Maehr, 1985; Maehr & Braskamp, 1986). Thus, even at this early stage of organizational evaluation and assessment, there is good reason to believe in the ultimate worth of an information based approach in building the organization into a smoothly functioning organism in which the separate parts are truly invested in the overall functions and goals. Data very seldom tell a manager specifically what to do, but they are very often the first step and a necessary step in the process (Braskamp & Brown, 1980). As managers consider production figures and ledger sheets, they also do well to view the health of the organizational culture. With increasing evidence that work motivation might be significantly determined by organizational culture, the necessity to systematically identify, assess, and evaluate this variable rightly becomes a significant concern at the highest levels of the organization.

Goal setting. Assessment lays a basis for action and for the evaluation of such actions. But what action might be taken? Goal setting clearly must be a focus of an organization if it is to exhibit the kind of sense of purpose that, as has been argued, is critical. This is not to suggest that there is available somewhere a "cookbook" on goal setting that you can employ and some mechanical procedures that you can easily put into practice for doing this although to some degree this is true. But, to make a more general point which is believed to be more adaptable to your individual situations, one does not have to create artificial situations in order to establish goals, purpose, and a broader understanding of why the organization exists. Meetings of the staff are a proper venue for goal concerns. Too often these meetings are merely concerned with trivia. But they can be important occasions for serious discussions of what the organization is and what it is to be. What kind of service does it provide? To whom does it give its service? What is the constituency? What is its unique role? What does it do that other groups cannot or do not do? How do various subgroups contribute to this overall purpose?

Those are the "ultimate goals." The penultimate goals are equally important. They relate to what kind of place we want this to be so we can get the job done. Do we have to have more or fewer meetings? Do we have to recognize good work more? Do we have to cooperate more?

In short, the overall point here is that in order to establish goals, purpose, and a mission one first has to engage the organization in goal talk. Second, one has to get a significant number of persons involved in specifying what the organization is about.

If any one technique for doing this should be emphasized, developing a strategic plan of some sort would be the one. The plan itself is not as important as the process of writing it. Through the years students have said that they really know some things but that they have a hard time writing them down. This author's response has been: you don't know anything until you can—maybe until you do—write it down. The process of operationalizing a collection of vague thoughts has an importance all of its own. Especially in establishing goals within an organization, writing a mission statement—a set of goals or a strategic plan—is an occasion for at least beginning to establish answers to the purpose of the organization, answers which relate to the meaning of why one should be personally invested in and committed to the organization.

Evaluation

There are few better ways of expressing what is expected than through the evaluation process and the reward and recognition that accompany this process. In attempting to foster organizational change of almost any type, the domain of reward and recognition must be extensively considered. Of course many managers personally evaluate the performance of only a few and certainly do not administer or actualize the evaluation process in a specific or direct way in many cases. But they do play a major role in establishing what is valued. They also set the tone for how evaluation is to be accomplished. In these two respects they can communicate the broad goals and mission of the organization.

To be a bit more concrete about this: Managers can choose to concern themselves with setting up systematic evaluation procedures and stress certain criteria. The mere fact that he/she establishes a group to do this and gives it some visibility may itself be sufficient to make it clear that there is concern and interest not only in evaluation but in certain performance criteria. Most important of all, doubtless, is that the manager must be seen to act in terms of the evaluation information. They must take it seriously and be recognized for doing so. In one form of the evaluation process—performance appraisal—it is clear that one can communicate what is expected through indicating an association between performance and reward (see, for example, Lawler, 1971; 1977).

Evaluation and assessment are integral parts of management style. Evaluation implies a caring and an interest in what is being accomplished. Not to evaluate is to imply indifference. Evaluation, although at times painful and difficult to do, has several important consequences. It provides an occasion for articulating the goals and mission of the organization for specific programs, persons, and units. The mere fact that evaluation occurs indicates that the organization cares about what is done. Properly done, evaluation can also reflect a concern for the growth of the individual worker as a contributor to the organization and suggest a stance that is generally growth oriented rather than static. It is through a concern with evaluation tht leaders affect the organizational culture. It is one of the buttons they can press for action in this regard.

Summary

In brief, this author wishes to stress the overwhelming importance for the leadership to be concerned with goals. The strategies alluded to earlier are really all a part of one whole. The whole concerns developing a set of shared goals which guide the operations of the organization. There is little question but that commitment—personal investment—is likely only as such a shared sense of purpose is extant within an organization.

CONCLUSION

There should be little doubt in anyone's mind that a sense of purpose is key to the development of personal investment in an organization. What may be less clear is the leader's role in this regard—a role which is both critical and problematic.

Leadership is critical to the establishment of a sense of what the organization is about. The leader is certainly not the only person involved in establishing purpose in the organization. But someone in a leadership role is inevitably critical in this regard. Someone has to initiate the process. Someone has to assess what is going on and project this into a sense of direction and purpose. Someone has to conceptualize, symbolize, and communicate the meaning and purpose of an organization. And that quite logically often is the formally designated leader of the organization.

But the role is problematic. To begin to articulate a set of goals and purposes, one has to go a bit beyond the information given. One does not have purpose handed to them on a silver platter. In helping an organization define purpose, leaders take a bit of a risk. Is this really a viable way to conceptualize what this group is about? Is it really acceptable both to the group and its constituency? Will it work? To the point: moderate risk-taking is implied in the role of leadership described earlier. That implies something about the kinds of persons that can and should be leaders. Perhaps that is a fitting note on which to conclude a talk to leaders about what is an important facet of their leadership function.

REFERENCES

Braskamp, L. A., & Brown, R. D. (Eds.). (1980). *Utilization of evaluation information.* San Francisco, CA: Jossey-Bass.

Braskamp, L. A., & Maehr, M. L. (1985). *Spectrum: An organizational development tool.* Champaign, IL: Metritech.

Hackman, J. R., & Oldham, G. R. (1980). *Work redesign.* Reading, MA: Addison-Wesley.

Maehr, M. L. (1987). Managing organizational culture to enhance motivation. In M. L. Maehr & D. A. Kleiber (Eds.), *Advances in motivation and achievement: A research annual. Vol. 5: Enhancing motivation* (pp. 287-320). Greenwich, CT: JAI Press.

Maehr, M. L., & Braskamp, L. A. (1986). *The motivation factor: A theory of personal investment.* Lexington, MA: Lexington Books.

McClelland, D. C. (1978). Managing motivation to expand human freedom. *American Psychologist, 33*(March), 201-210.

McClelland, D. C., & Winter, D. G. (1971). *Motivating economic achievement.* New York: Free Press.

NORMAN HOLMAN

Deputy Director
Cleveland Public Library
Cleveland, Ohio

Collective Bargaining in Public Libraries: Preserving Management Prerogatives

ABSTRACT

Drawing mostly from the history of public sector collective bargaining in Ohio, laws and chronology are examined for insight into the importance of management rights and prerogatives. Special attention is given to dispute resolution and the respective rights of management and labor in it, since the existence of a dispute is likely to reveal an issue where one or the other party may acquire previously undefined authority.

INTRODUCTION

Collective bargaining, or its absence, has been governed for years in Ohio by the Ferguson Act. The Ferguson Act was enacted in 1943 in direct response to numerous crippling strikes in the private sector following World War II. The law was sweeping and unambiguous. All strikes in the public sector were outlawed. The stated penalties for striking public employees were severe; the act provided for termination of employment for failure to end illegal strikes. It further provided that illegal strikers could not receive increased compensation for one year following an illegal strike and included probation for a like period.

The law held firm and intact for many years, but in the 1960s and early 1970s public employees in Ohio, as in many other states, began to organize and seek representation at the bargaining table. In 1975, deciding on a case referred to as the Dayton Classroom Teachers Association *v.* Dayton Board of Education, the Ohio Supreme Court held that public employees could meet and negotiate binding collective bargaining agreements with employers. The court also held, however, that

11

employees have no constitutional right to require their employers to bargain collectively.

In the following years, collective bargaining spread unimpeded to most of the public sector employment throughout Ohio. Public libraries, however, seemed not to have been affected. Perhaps the wealth bestowed upon many public libraries by the intangible personal property tax (imposed on stocks and investments) induced satisfaction or complacency among library employees. Staff associations, in their roles as social organizers and combined with benign advocacy, may have participated sufficiently in organizations' governance. The exception was the Public Library of Youngstown and Mahoning County, an association library under Ohio laws, which had a collective bargaining agreement for years under the jurisdiction of the National Labor Relations Board, since a state labor relations authority had not existed until the recently enacted Ohio Public Employees Collective Bargaining Act.

The first drafts of the Ohio Public Employees Collective Bargaining Act (the act), Chapter 4117 of the *Ohio Revised Code*, were considered in 1971, a year after the neighboring state of Pennsylvania passed its collective bargaining bill. After a 1973 senate defeat and vetoes in 1975 and 1977 by then Governor James Rhodes, Governor Richard Celeste signed the bill into law on July 6, 1983. The act became effective on April 1, 1984.

Ohio became the thirty-ninth state to pass a public sector labor law. One might have expected Ohio to be among the first group of states to do this because of its extensive labor history in the private sector with steelworkers, autoworkers, and the Teamsters. By the time Ohio had passed a public sector labor law, the legislature was essentially catching up with history. Collective bargaining in the public sector in fact had been established for years. Among other accomplishments, the act created a regulatory body in the form of the State Employment Relations Board (SERB). SERB was accorded authority to make rules for executing the act, which has not been a small task in light of the large amount of public sector collective bargaining that preceded its existence.

The point here is not to list and summarize the act in Ohio but to draw from it as a source for discussing bargaining procedures including dispute resolution and subjects of bargaining in public libraries. A discussion of dispute resolution procedures leads inevitably to a consideration of strikes in the public sector—who can and who cannot strike— and the inclusion of public libraries among those employers where strikes are permitted.

DISPUTE RESOLUTION PROCEDURES

Bargaining typically is initiated by a notice of at least sixty days prior to expiration of an existing contract or the date termination or modification of an existing contract is to be effective. Initial negotiations must be conducted for a minimum of ninety days, according to the Ohio Act, before dispute resolution procedures apply.

The parties can mutually agree upon dispute resolution procedures, which would supersede the procedures mandated by the act; that is, provided the procedures negotiated lead to final resolution and not merely to mediation. If the parties cannot agree to a dispute resolution procedure, the one specified in the act will apply. Objectionable to the employer in most state mandated impasse procedures is the inclusion of fact-finding following mediation.

In state mandated impasse procedures, Ohio being a typical example, SERB will appoint a mediator to assist the parties in the process of collective bargaining. The mediator's sole function is to reconcile differences between the parties which may take the form of: (1) settlement of the overall agreement; (2) reduction in the number of overall issues; or (3) narrowing of the differences on the open issues without completely resolving them. The mediator will have only a brief time, fourteen days, within which to work magic. If the mediator reports to the state agency that impasse still exists, a fact-finding panel will be appointed.

Fact-finding is a process that requires the parties at a hearing to present evidence to a neutral fact-finder supporting their respective positions on outstanding issues. Usually the fact-finder must meet with both parties' approval unless the parties cannot agree in which case the state agency would select the panel. In some states, such as New York, the state agency makes the selection without input from the parties (New York Public Employees' Fair Employment Act, 1985a).

During fact-finding, each party provides the fact-finder with statements, probably written, specifying the unresolved issues and the parties' position on each. The panel makes final recommendations as to all unresolved issues. Either party may reject the fact-finder's recommendations. Since the fact-finder's recommendations either will be adopted or, if not, will have set the stage for a strike or interest arbitration, they are not subject to judicial review.

Specific elements of fact-finding facilitate impasse resolution. Fact-finding is a more formal process than either negotiations or mediation because the parties must prepare rational arguments supporting their positions to submit to the fact-finder at a hearing. The strength or weakness of the rationale significantly affects the outcome. Fact-finding is effective because it may have the power of persuading the parties to move from relatively unreasonable positions to the reasonable solutions recommended by the fact-finder. Furthermore, weakness in the parties' positions is exposed through cross-examination, presentation of evidence by the other party, and through inquiry by the fact-finder. Fact-finding also carries the power of the final step before a strike, which is the terminal step in statutory impasse procedures and may impose costs that both parties view as unacceptable.

Voluntary dispute resolution procedures in states where the parties have the option of agreeing to them are usually preferred. As stated earlier, provided the procedure leads to final resolution, the parties are able to forge a method of resolving impasse that suits each party's individual and collective circumstances. Procedures could include: (1) conventional arbitration of all unsettled issues, in which case the arbitrator is not limited to a choice between the last offers of the parties; (2) arbitration limited to a choice between the last offer of each party as either single package or on each issue submitted; or (3) any other settlement procedures agreed to by the parties. The parties may include the right to strike except those that are involved in safety-related jobs which are usually prohibited from striking.

Methods involving arbitration probably would be rejected in situations where the parties are confident in their abilities to resolve impasse on their own and where arbitrarily imposed solutions are unacceptable. As an example, Cleveland Public Library, Cleveland, Ohio, and District 925, Service Employees International Union, during their negotiations that began in May 1987, mutually agreed not to follow the dispute resolution procedure provided by the Ohio Public Employees Collective Bargaining Act and substituted their own procedure as permitted in Chapter 4117 of the *Ohio Revised Code*.

During negotiations, the parties expressed or implied that neither wanted the delay and cost involved with fact-finding. Furthermore, the library bargaining committee did not want publication of the fact-finder's recommendations resulting from fact-finding. Neither the library nor District 925 wanted to refer the matter of impasse to a SERB appointed mediator, and the Cleveland Public Library in particular did not want to have its economic fate, should economic issues be among those at impasse, determined by a third party.

If the parties had followed the procedure available under the statute, they could have agreed to resolve the economic impasse by means of interest arbitration, and the arbitrator would determine the economic issue or issues presented by the parties. For a publicly supported institution with a fixed budget, the risks connected with interest arbitration outweighed the advantages of following such a procedure.

Under the Alternative Dispute Resolution between the library and District 925 (discussed later), the parties could bargain for as long as five months, in contrast to the ninety day period under the statute, prior to either party's having the right to request the Federal Mediation and Conciliation Service to appoint a federal mediator. It is interesting that the parties agreed also that an actual impasse did not have to exist for either party to request a mediator, rather that "the differences of position are so substantial that further negotiations may not produce a satisfactory agreement." "Impasse" suggests deadlock, which may not be present in the situation characterized in the procedure.

ALTERNATIVE DISPUTE RESOLUTION PROCEDURE

1. The dispute settlement procedure set forth in this agreement shall

govern negotiations conducted between the Employer and the Union and shall be the agreement of the parties hereto and shall supersede the procedures set forth in *Ohio Revised Code* 4117.14 and related sections and regulations.

2. When tentative agreement is reached through negotiations, the tentative agreement shall be reduced to writing and shall be submitted to the Union membership for approval. After approval, the tentative agreement will be submitted for approval to the Employer. Each negotiating team shall urge and recommend approval of the tentative agreement.

3. If either party at any time after midnight *(date)* determines that the differences of position are so substantial that further negotiations may not produce a satisfactory agreement, either party may request the Federal Mediation and Conciliation Services (FMCS) to appoint a federal mediator for the purpose of assisting the parties in reaching an agreement.

4. If after thirty days from the first meeting with a federal mediator the Union believes that negotiations cannot be resolved through the procedure outlined earlier, it may engage in a strike upon ten days written notice to the Employer and to the State Employment Relations Board (Cleveland Public Library District 925. Service Employees International Union, 1987, p. 1).

With due recognition to the time needed to obtain a federal mediator and schedule meetings, thirty days from the first meeting between the parties with a federal mediator must elapse before the union may engage in a strike, and then such a strike must be upon ten days written notice to the library and to SERB. The state mandated dispute resolution, which included fact-finding, and the alternative dispute resolution procedure, described and outlined earlier, include the union's right to strike upon notice to the employer and SERB in the event the parties fail to reach an agreement. Only safety forces in Ohio are not permitted to strike even after exhaustion of bargaining, mediation, and fact-finding. All states are not the same in their positions on whether public employees have the right to strike. In Massachusetts and New York, for example, the law prohibits public employees from striking (Annotated Laws of Massachusetts, 1983; New York Public Employees Fair Employment Act, 1985b). In all states that permit public employees to strike, however, none seems to include librarians among those prohibited as safety forces or otherwise from striking.

While the arguments pro and con regarding the union's right to strike in the public sector are familiar to many, they bear repeating for the benefit of the uninitiated and as a review for the rest:

Pro:

1. Public employees are entitled to the same rights accorded private employees.

2. The right of public employees to engage in collective bargaining is meaningless unless supported by some mechanism for clout such as a strike.
3. Strikes are an effective extension of the collective bargaining process, do not occur frequently enough to justify their prohibition, and generally are not harmful to public health, safety, or welfare.

Con:
Public and private sectors are very different and public sector employees are therefore not entitled to the same rights accorded private sector employees.

1. Public employees provide unique and essential services.
2. Private sector market forces are missing from the public sector.
3. Strikes may damage public health, safety, and welfare.

Once notification has been given that a strike will occur, the public employer is empowered to seek injunctive or court ordered relief. Injunctive relief is unequivocal where the strike is illegal, such as during pendency of the act's settlement procedure or during the term of the collective bargaining agreement in states where such strikes are clearly prohibited by law. Even under circumstances of a legal strike, the employer may seek a restraining order while continuing to bargain, which would usually be assisted by a mediator. Such restraint on the public employees' right to strike would have to be preceded by the finding that a strike may pose clear and present danger to the health or safety of the public.

INTEREST ARBITRATION

In discussing the rationale for an Alternative Dispute Resolution Procedure between Cleveland Public Library and District 925, interest arbitration was characterized as a risky option to resolve economic impasse. In interest arbitration a designated neutral party is used to determine future contract terms which will bind the parties who have been unable to achieve a new agreement through the bargaining process (Elkouri & Elkouri, 1973, pp. 47-50). Interest arbitrators generally possess liberal authority to formulate the actual employment terms which will govern the relationship of parties who have been unable to achieve a voluntary agreement themselves (Overton, 1973, pp. 159-66). Although interest arbitration—also known as final offer settlement, conciliation, or mandatory arbitration—is mandatory for safety forces, anyone covered by the act may agree to such a settlement procedure.

Interest arbitration is conducted by a conciliator who must conduct a hearing as soon as practicable. By a given period of time each party must submit a written report summarizing the unresolved issues, the party's final offer, and the rationale for that position. The conciliator, in turn, selects, issue-by-issue, the final settlement offer of one of the parties. The conciliator by Ohio law cannot suggest a compromise position.

Interest arbitration carries risks for both parties and generates, of necessity, serious policy considerations. Interest arbitration may delegate policy-making authority illegally to an unelected person or board that is not designated by the statutes to perform a particular function. Boards of Library Trustees for public libraries in Ohio are accorded vast powers to set policy for their respective institutions. Specifically mentioned in the *Ohio Revised Code* 3375.40 is the authority to "appoint and fix" compensation. Economic issues resolved through interest arbitration appear to circumvent the appropriate authority to set compensation and related benefits such as sick leave. Since a conciliator's decisions may impose an untenable economic burden on the library, the subsequent adjustments to spending priorities and probable need to generate additional revenue also may violate equal protection, since the effect would be to shift improperly to a person or board the power to tax.

There are other arguments less esoteric than apparently constitutional issues to be leveled against interest arbitration. From the employer's vantage point, interest arbitration may result in administrative awards of unaffordable wages. From the vantage point of both parties it is a risk to have a third party write the contract who is unfamiliar with the practicalities of the shared situation. Perhaps of greatest significance, however, is that it damages collective bargaining because the parties ultimately fail to bargain. The process does not encourage cooperation; rather it tends to push the parties apart and separates them from their mutual concerns. Only when strikes are prohibited—such as for safety forces, and the state must provide a substitute for resolving impasses—is interest arbitration desirable. States where collective bargaining is permitted in the public sector recognize that there should be no work stoppages of services that may endanger the health and safety of the public.

MANAGEMENT RIGHTS

Collective bargaining, by its nature, limits management rights. In the place of unimpeded management rights is a contract which restricts both parties in the exercise of their respective rights and obligates both parties to act in responsible ways.

As a subject of bargaining, management rights are regarded as both mandatory and permissive. Typical mandatory subjects of bargaining are wages, hours, other conditions of the contract, and changes in existing provisions of a collective bargaining agreement. Management rights are mandatory to the extent they affect wages, hours, and terms and conditions of employment. Typical permissive subjects of bargaining are the method of recording minutes of bargaining sessions and benefits of retirees. To the extent that there may be areas remaining where management rights can be exercised at all, they are a permissive subject and are in the category of those for which only the parties may bargain. In many contracts, management rights outside the mandatory subjects would be reserved in all areas of responsibility "except where otherwise provided."

In Ohio, management rights are itemized under the list of permissive subjects included in the act. These are:

1. Determine matters of inherent managerial policy which include, but are not limited to, areas of discretion or policy such as the functions and programs of the employer, standards of services, its overall budget, utilization of technology, and organization structure;
2. direct, supervise, evaluate, or hire employees;
3. maintain and improve the efficiency and effectiveness of governmental operations;
4. determine the overall methods, process, means, or personnel by which governmental operations are to be conducted;
5. suspend, discipline, demote, or discharge for just cause, or lay off, transfer, assign, schedule, promote, or retain employees;
6. determine the adequacy of the work force;
7. determine the overall mission of the employer as a unit of government;
8. effectively manage the work force; and
9. take actions to carry out the mission of the employer as a govenmental unit (*Ohio Revised Code*, 1987).

The presence of detail in the act outlining management rights suggests that omissions may be deliberate and intended to be restrictive. Whether that is true or not, management must establish rights to create rules, policies, and practices in areas not mentioned by the act and in situations arising during the life of the contract not anticipated by the act or the bargained contract. Practically, management must assume responsibility in those areas anyway because it will be held accountable for resolving the problems such situations may generate. To that end, as an addendum to management rights, the following language not found in Ohio's Act would ensure management's ability to be responsive:

> The exercise of the foregoing rights, and the adoption of reasonable policies, rules, and practices in furtherance thereof, shall be limited only by the specific terms of this Agreement and pertinent statutes, and then only to the extent such specific terms hereof are in conformance with the Constitution and laws of the State and of the United States (Cleveland Public Library and District 925, Service Employees International. Union, 1987, p. 4)

The exercise of management rights, even those seemingly protected by laws and a collective bargaining agreement, evolves reluctantly. Acting in the interest of the institution it safeguards, management's good intentions may be thwarted by the legitimate rights of its employees.

Management's responsibility to act—for example, against drug abuse in the workplace and its right to create policy that establishes a drug free environment—must be weighed against employees' right to privacy. The possession, use, and sale of drugs on library premises clearly are criminal acts. Employers have a right and responsibility to halt criminal activity. To protect the rights of all employees to work in a hassle-free environment, the employer has a right and responsibility to eliminate unruly behavior that accompanies illegal drug abuse. Furthermore, employees whose skills are impaired by the presence of drugs can pose a health and safety threat to themselves, fellow employees, and the public. Everyone who is prudent and reasonable should recognize the management's right to prohibit possession, use, and sale of illegal drugs in the workplace.

For the sake of argument, imagine an employer that believes that efforts to deter drug use are more effective when detection and therapy are available during the early stages of drug use. Such a judgment could be made for purely humanitarian reasons, totally lacking in nefarious motives, and because there is an interest in identifying and correcting individuals' drug abuse before it is manifested in significant performance shortcomings. Since employees have no right to possess, sell, or use illegal drugs in any environment, including the workplace, and employers have a legitimate right to prohibit employees' possession, sale, and use of illegal drugs, the employer may have sound reasons to conclude that drug testing is an effective means to therapeutic intervention.

The implementation of drug testing would inspire opposition from labor advocates and representatives on the grounds that it violates employees' rights to privacy and perpetuates discrimination against the handicapped and Title VII discrimination. Furthermore, they would argue from the employer's standpoint that it invites wrongful discharge suits. All of that may be true, one argues, but management rights are stifled if such a clearly pernicious problem as drug abuse cannot be addressed by the rightful party which is management.

The National Labor Relations Board (NLRB) recently issued a complaint against an employer that unilaterally implemented a drug testing program (National Labor Relations Board, 1987). State labor relations agencies are likely to fashion similar decisions in their respective jurisdictions. In fact, a regulatory agency, such as the NLRB or a state board, could require, in a unionized workplace, that the parties should meet and bargain in good faith on the subjects of drug testing or employee assistance programs (EAP). Because the consideration of these policies and practices would constitute the change in a condition of employment and the subsequent modification or deletion of an existing provision of the collective bargaining agreement, it becomes a mandatory subject of bargaining, and adhering to a claim of management rights on the subject of unilateral implementation would be futile. The parties must bargain.

Employee and management cooperation can be difficult to achieve. In many workplaces, joint employee and management committees provide the method by which employers effectively solicit employees' concerns and, where it is appropriate, include them in the decision-making. It is typical that negotiated agreements contain specific provision for committees to work on subjects of health and safety and position classification. Some contracts provide for the formation of a general committee with sweeping responsibilities limited only by an understanding that contract interpretation and pending grievances are forbidden subjects. These committees can be productive vehicles for solving problems and addressing contentious issues before they become problems. They may generate a cooperative approach to shared concerns, assuming their processes do not deteriorate into institutionalized value bashing, and successfully ameliorate the traditional adversarial relationship between employees and management in the public library.

REFERENCES

Annotated laws of Massachusetts. (1983). Chapter 150E, Section 9 (A).

Cleveland Public Library and District 925, Service Employees International Union. (1987). *Alternative dispute resolution: Proposed contract language.* May 28.

Cleveland Public Library and District 925, Service Employees International Union. (1987). *Agreement Between Cleveland Public Library and District 25.* April 12.

Elkouri, F., & Elkouri, E. A. (1973). *How arbitration works* (4th Ed.). Washington, DC: Bureau of National Affairs.

National Labor Relations Board. (1987). Pratt vs. Whitney. Case No. 39, CA 3263. June 3.

New York Public Employees' Fair Employment Act. (1985a). Section 209 (3) (b).

New York Public Employees' Fair Employment Act. (1985b). Section 210 (1).

Ohio Revised Code. (1987). Section 4117.08 (C).

Overton, C. E. (1973). Criterion in grievance and interest arbitration in the public sector. *Arbitration Journal, 28,* 159-166.

KATHLEEN M. HEIM

Dean
School of Library and Information Science
Louisiana State University
Baton Rouge, Louisiana

Organizational Entry: Human Resources Selection and Adaptation in Response to a Complex Labor Pool

ABSTRACT

Entry-level recruitment to library organizations is discussed in light of the complex labor pool. Suggestions are provided for better techniques to accommodate both employer and employee goals. The need for clearer articulation of specializations to facilitate targeted preparation of new entrants is presented as a strategy to develop a broader cadre of entry-level personnel.

INTRODUCTION

The complexity of the labor pool comprised of individuals holding an accredited degree in library and information science presents special problems regarding organizational entry. This article examines three topics: (1) the complexity of the labor pool; (2) the scope of organizational entry considerations; and (3) considerations for organizational entry in a library and information environment.

Historically, the *organization* has been the focus of study regarding recruitment of personnel. That is, individuals have been seen in terms of how they will fit into an organization, what skills and abilities they bring, and how they will be trained. Recently, some researchers have begun to consider the process from the dual perspective of the organization and the individual. Wanous (1980, p. 10) has proposed a matching process that considers the needs of human beings and the capacity of organizations to meet those needs. While the traditional view of organizational selection is that an individual's abilities should meet the organization's job requirements—resulting in good job performance—a more expansive view is that the needs of individuals and the organization's

21

capacity to reinforce those needs, results in job satisfaction and commitment to the organization. *Needs* represent basic strivings, and *abilities* represent what people can or are able to do. Clearly the individual is concerned with the former and the organization with the latter. The challenge of successful recruitment is to strike a balance between the two.

THE COMPLEXITY OF THE LABOR POOL FOR LIBRARY AND INFORMATION SCIENCE POSITIONS

For simplicity, this discussion considers only first positions. Mid-level and upper-management positions involve different sets of norms and factors relating to occupational culture and require separate analysis. Dailey (1982) has posited that a completely new personnel selection system is required at these levels based upon "track record inquiry." However, since recruitment at higher levels requires a considerably different set of factors (including, but not limited to, institutional comparability, career stage development, and professional affiliation), this discussion will focus on the composition of the labor pool for the first position.

Since most accredited programs of library and information science education grant an "all-purpose" degree, it might be assumed by employers at the outset that the potential labor pool for any entry-level position is fairly homogeneous. However, this is certainly not the case. Most new graduates with mobility target public service in an academic library as their most desirable job (Heim & Moen, 1989). Each program will graduate a few students with clear and specific career goals based, usually, upon preprofessional experience—such as health sciences libraries or music librarianship—but most new graduates will modify career goals in light of constraints on mobility, available positions, and recruitment strategies of potential employers.

The primary fact to keep in mind is that each employer will find a different labor pool for different jobs subject to many variables. A few examples will illustrate this.

—A large urban public library with no library education program in the local metropolitan area will experience difficulty in identifying youth services personnel for an entry-level post.

—A small academic library in a small town will experience little difficulty in attracting candidates for a public services position.

—An urban academic library with library education attainable through part-time or full-time study will find it relatively easy to obtain candidates for most entry-level positions.

—School library positions—in states where the accredited degree is not a requisite for employment—will not be difficult to fill if teacher education programs provide state required courses.

—Large urban libraries—whether academic or public—will experience difficulty in hiring if cost of living is extraordinarily high.

—Suburban communities, in areas where there is no library education program, will experience difficulty in hiring entry-level personnel especially for public library positions.

Far more than we like to admit, mobility plays a great part in the candidate pool for entry-level positions. Because the median age of new graduates is high—mid-thirties—many have already begun families or made commitments to given communities, drastically cutting back the pool of mobile candidates for entry-level positions. Because entry-level salaries are low, relocation is generally based mainly upon an impacted local labor market. A good case in point is this author's experience of recent graduates at Louisiana State University. Until recently, local entry-level salaries were extremely low—$3,000-$4,000 below the national average. Consequently, graduates with mobility tended to relocate. However, recent salary increases in the local job market closer to the national average have tended to keep a larger portion of new graduates in the state—even those from other regions. Whereas a $3,000 to $4,000 differential was impetus to move, a differential of $1,000 to $2,000 was not, given that entry level positions seldom provide moving expenses—and often do not even provide interview reimbursement.

Additionally, when graduates move they tend to move for positions they perceive (rightly or wrongly) as providing potential for growth and advancement. Thus the public services positions in academic libraries are pursued as these seem to hold promise for careers and development. Positions that candidates view as somewhat static (such as youth services or technical services) do not draw a large and geographically diverse labor pool. A solid example of this would be school library media positions. While an individual may move for such a position, this is generally due to family relocation—*not* due to the candidate perusing openings throughout the nation and then applying. (Compounding this problem is the school systems' own tendency to hire and promote from within and to prefer less experienced candidates due to costs.)

Available Positions

To a large degree, those graduates without clear career goals are rather open-ended as to first job. For those with no mobility, career goals are flexible enough to modify the job search to meet local labor needs. Again, to use the example of Louisiana State University, few matriculated students enter the program with the idea of service in state libraries or state agencies. However, the proximity of state government means that such positions are available and are generally filled by new graduates. Although the state library regularly advertises its positions in the national press, the salaries are not high enough to attract many distance candidates and the labor needs are largely met through hiring nonmobile new graduates.

It seems that students will modify their course of study for the jobs that they perceive as desirable. "Online searching" and "bibliographic instruction" courses attract students who are targeting public service positions in academic libraries, but few students will enroll in our "management of technical service" seminars. There is a break between students' perceived ideas of positions and their desire to prepare for positions. While those in the public services career stream can take little credit for the fact that many students will modify their studies to meet job requirements, it remains true that this appears to be the only reasonably well understood career stream on the part of most students. This is probably due to the visibility of these positions during undergraduate or other graduate study.

What is needed to generate career orientation toward the requirements of the employing libraries is a profession-wide commitment to delineating career paths for areas of library service in which there is a shortfall of new entrants. While those in library education try to convey the career potential of youth services or technical services, there is not enough provision of role models in the field whose careers have been analyzed to make such specialization attractive. Thus most new graduates will accept these perceived less desirable positions for reasons other than career commitment.

Employer Response to a Complex Labor Pool

Employers who are disappointed at a small candidate pool for new positions may not realize that positions outside of public service require a different recruitment strategy than simply placing an advertisement in the national press. However, once the factors of mobility and accommodation of new entrants to available positions are understood, employers should be able to develop a recruitment plan that enables them to attract a broader selection of applicants. Techniques for managing recruitment in light of a complex labor pool will be discussed in the third section of this article.

THE SCOPE OF ORGANIZATIONAL ENTRY CONSIDERATIONS

Activities Prior to Recruitment

"Organizational entry" refers to those components of the hiring process that surround an individual's recruitment, selection, and socialization. Before any contact is made with candidates for employment, each position—whether newly created or ongoing—should first be subjected to job analysis. Without a complete job analysis prior to selection-related activities, the entire organizational entry process can be jeopardized.

A number of well-developed techniques exist for the conduct of an effective job analysis. These include: (1) *Job Analysis Interviews*—a trained analyst collects data by studying employees familiar with the job under consideration; (2) *Task Analysis Inventories*—questionnaires listing tasks associated with the open position that define the principal tasks for a given job; (3) *Position Analysis Questionnaires*— standardized evaluation tools that examine work activities and compensation issues; (4) *Guidelines Oriented Job Analysis*—a multistep process designed to develop a selection plan reflecting the job being studied; (5) *the Iowa Merit Employment Systems*—a process designed to lead to content-valid selection devices; (6) *Functional Job Analysis*—a thorough procedure for applying a standardized controlled language for describing and measuring what workers do on a job; and (7) *The Job Element Method* which is designed to identify the characteristics of superior workers on the job (Feild & Gatewood, 1987, pp. 113-22).

In their article, "Matching Talent with the Task," Feild and Gatewood (1987, pp. 122-24) compare these methods of job analysis in light of the *EEOC Uniform Guidelines on Employee Selection Procedure* which lay out legal reasons for using job analysis as part of a selection program. They also compare the seven methods on twelve variables: (1) operational currency; (2) degree to which the methodological instruments are directly usable; (3) occupational versatility; (4) standardization; (5) acceptability to users/respondents; (6) required amount of job analyst training; (7) sample size; (8) suitability for content validity; (9) suitability for criterion-related validity; (10) reliability; (11) utility in developing selection measures; and (12) cost.

The need for job analysis is underscored in Isacco and Smith's (1985) assertion that one of the primary reasons that the hiring process fails is due to lack of attention to prerecruitment activities. In their review, they observe that the spectrum of organizational policies relating to personnel should be surveyed frequently to avoid legal problems and to ensure that the job analysis procedure takes place with appropriate attention to position and organizational requirements.

Once the new position is sufficiently clear to those who will be involved in hiring, internal selection procedures should be established. These will vary depending upon the level of position. As noted before, procedures and recruitment for mid or upper-level positions are different enough from entry-level positions to warrant consideration other than that which is the focus of this article.

Stages in Entry
For entry-level professional positions, however, there are special problems associated with the transition from college to work that need to be considered. The model developed by Phillips (1987) is especially helpful.

Phillips's discussion focuses upon organizational entry to professional jobs. Although the model he presents does not differ, on first glance, from traditional models of entry, his focus on those aspects of the process of particular import to new employees who have just completed their professional education has great relevance for this discussion (Phillips, 1987, pp. 35-42). In brief, the stages include:

—*Recruitment:* This is the period in which employers work to ensure a good match between individuals and jobs. Particular schools may be identified that are known to produce ideal candidates. However, employers should not oversell their organization in such a way that new hires are disappointed upon entering the organization.

—*Pre-employment education:* Given the amount of time between selection and entry, this stage can vary greatly. However, a number of activities that can provide early introduction to the organizational culture can be executed that provide for better transition. These include provision of publications (annual reports, in-house newsletters), direct communications from key people (such as memos that would be routed to the new employees if they were already on the job), or job related documents such as policy manuals.

—*Orientation:* This begins upon arrival to the new position. Well-planned orientations with clear goals and objectives should take advantage of new graduates' enthusiasm. Initial perceptions of colleagues and culture make the strongest impact at this time. Attitudes may be shaped if organizational goals are made clear.

—*Education/training:* These activities are aimed at preparing the new employee to accommodate pre-entry education to actual position requirements. These activities should be organized with the needs of both the individual and organization's in mind.

—*Adaptation:* This is the stage at which an individual through recruitment, pre-employment interaction, orientation, and education/training has adopted the culture of the organization. Performance feedback is crucial to good adaptation.

—*Promotion/assignment:* Many organizations bring in strong new graduates with the intent of placing them where they are best suited once initial stages are completed. It is critical to make the first assignment to positions in which individuals are challenged and well-motivated.

—*Evaluation:* This relates to an overall assessment of the management of the transition and is a mechanism for gauging the effectiveness of the methods employed in earlier stages.

Each stage of the organizational entry process can be configured to meet the requirements of a given organization as well as to the individual position. What needs to be kept in mind at all times, however, is that this is a process that can be managed and must be managed if the organization is to be successful in identifying and retaining excellent employees. The costs of hiring—both actual and in terms of personnel time expended—are so great that organizational entry is the most crucial aspect of human resources management.

ADDITIONAL CONSIDERATIONS FOR ORGANIZATIONAL ENTRY IN A LIBRARY AND INFORMATION ENVIRONMENT

How Library and Information Science Entry Differs

How do we superimpose general organizational entry considerations onto the complex labor pool for library and information science positions? First, we need to delineate how this labor pool differs from the general labor pool to which most of the organizational entry literature is directed, and how library organizations differ from other large organizations vis-à-vis their approach to career development.

As described in section one, a very small percentage of new graduates consciously target their graduate education for "a technical services post in a major academic library" or a "youth services position in a suburban public library." Unlike the MBA graduate who prepares generically for a "management position in a large corporation," and looks to the employment market in terms of organizational status and long-term security, the typical MLIS graduate is far more constrained by external factors such as mobility and perceived availability of career development within an organization. While the large corporation accommodates this generic approach through the transition stages outlined in section two—that is taking the best raw talent and reassigning it to posts where skills and organizational needs mesh—library employers recruit for a specific position and thus limit the chances that a new employee will develop innate skills.

Compounding this is the fact that top positions in library and information science are rarely achieved through excellence in one organization. Recent studies have shown that high achievers in academic librarianship exhibit mobility and, in fact, must plan to move several times to different organizations if they are to be appointed to top administrative levels (Anderson, 1985).

This is quite different from other types of organizations that consciously work to develop career ladders within an organization and thus may be more inclined to invest larger amounts of organizational resources in employee education and assignation.

A Functional Approach to Library and Information Science Entry

Each individual library administration must certainly develop its own entry process comprised of the components already described. However, the field must take a more concerted stance vis-à-vis some aspects of this process because a given library is not just recruiting for its own needs but for the needs of its entire type of function. Taking this view, which is based upon a more realistic understanding of the potential new-entrant labor pool, there are different explications that might be used to describe some of the stages in Phillips's model. Some of these that consider entry are suggested later—not from a specific library's vantage, but from the vantage of the field as a whole or at least from that of a type of library or function.

Recruitment. This aspect of employment has long been viewed to lesser or greater degrees as a profession-wide responsibility. Recent shortages for many specializations such as technical processes or youth services have combined to create profession-wide concern (Heim, 1988, pp. 7-9).

This concern has manifested itself in the establishment of recruitment committees within the American Library Association's various sections as well as through ongoing programs of the association's Office for Library Personnel Resources. In response to this concern, the focus of National Library Week in 1989 was the "information professional," with the intent of demonstrating the importance of librarians to information provision as well as the viability of information service as a career.

The "recruitment" process must necessarily include recruitment to the field as well as from the field. Although most employers are looking to fill a specific job opening, they must keep in mind the reasons that the candidate pool may be disappointingly small. Foremost of these reasons include low salaries. New college graduates today are more oriented to economic rewards. If entry-level salaries continue lower than salaries paid to teachers (who require only a baccalaureate degree), it is unlikely that new graduates will choose to enter a masters degree program without better economic incentive. A first step in achieving a larger labor pool is to raise salaries to a level wherein the library and information science profession can compete with other professions. While individual libraries may choose to raise salaries to be competitive for the new mobile graduates, this is a matter of libraries competing against each other and does not address the systemic problem of the field's overall unattractiveness due to low starting pay.

As a library and information science education program dean, this author receives many requests in the course of a year to consider curricular changes. These requests usually come from committees of professional associations. Typically, model programs are proposed for discrete specializations such as map librarianship, media cataloging, or service to the young adolescent. The reason that many specializations cannot receive attention has already been alluded to—few students enter programs with clear career goals. Certainly one reason for the requests to provide curricular exposure to specializations is that the requestors surmise that curricular exposure will lead to career interest. Unfortunately, this remedy cannot be all things to all areas in which shortages are occurring. Students must have a sense of what the specialization for which curricular change is requested can lead to—that is, what are the long-term career options of map librarianship, media cataloging, or service to the young adolescent?

Pre-employment education. The Phillips model views the period between the job offer and organizational entry as a time to begin the socialization to the employing institution. Certainly this holds true for an employing library, but in a broader sense it is time to socialize to the larger profession as well. Given the shortage of new graduates, we have found that some entrepreneurial employers are visiting campus and making offers very early to excellent candidates. With a longer pre-employment period, the new employee can turn some attention to accommodating the specialization for which they were hired. In three very different cases this year (health sciences, youth services, and public library/technical service) students hired early were supported by their future employer to attend local conferences in the area of specialization. This author also noted that these students are developing papers and independent studies in connection with their future work and, in one case, was taking adjunct courses that will be of use on the job.

Orientation. There are a number of excellent books and articles slated particularly to library orientation for new employees (Dewey, 1987; Creth, 1986). However, these tend, as does Phillips, to focus on organization-specific orientation. Clearly, in very small libraries, there may be no mechanism for internal career development. Obversely, in very large libraries, the mechanism for career development may well be through identification of a job in another similarly sized institution at a different level. Part of the orientation process should be a discussion of career issues that may not directly affect performance in the employing institution.

Also, given the "isolate" nature of specializations, individuals should be given some sanction to initiate interaction with specialists at other institutions. In a large academic library, the new cataloger assigned to Slavic cataloging should be affirmed in seeking and sustaining contact with Slavic experts at other institutions. In a small public library, the lone youth services specialist should be encouraged to meet on a regular basis with those at other libraries engaged in similar work.

Education/training. Most libraries are unlike large corporations wherein individuals may spend orientation time learning about the organization for an extended period. In libraries, many employees are given only a brief time for institutional orientation and are then expected to assume the responsibilities for which they have been hired. The carefully planned in-house education and training program advocated by Phillips has been formulated and is in place at many libraries (Creth, 1986; Hunt, 1983) but is not usually provided as part of the process of identification of the right person for the right job. Except at the largest libraries, individuals are hired for specific posts. One possible change for organizational entry in libraries—at least larger libraries—might be employment of excellent graduates with no specific job in mind but later job placement once an individual's strengths are assessed. This idea is not new (the Library of Congress Intern Program is a case in point), but broader acceptance of such a practice might be a workable alternative to job specific employment.

The profession is actually well positioned to foster intra-organizational adaptation through mechanisms such as the American

Library Association's divisions which provide functional or type-of-library career development through annual program meetings, opportunities to serve on committees with like-minded colleagues, and extensive journal publications. However, all of these opportunities are not available to all professionals due to cost or local barriers, and thus the pool of candidates adapted to the larger organizational culture may not be as large as employers would like. This, in turn, causes problems for recruitment to positions at higher levels.

Promotion/assignment. As was noted under the "Education/training" stage, few libraries províde an extended training period at the end of which an individual is assigned a post that best suits their talents and abilities. This may well be an area of human resources management for libraries in which work must be concentrated.

What would be the best situation for employers' seeking to fill library and information positions? Ideally, the field would attract large enough numbers of new entrants that employers would be able to delineate specific career preparations and would thus have a broad field from which to choose. Realistically, the small number of entrants and constraints already outlined, such as low salaries and unfocused position expectations at time of matriculation, means that students are unlikely in the aggregate to identify specific careers at the outset and consciously prepare for them.

So what compromise can be reached? This author suggests that, in the short-run, employers and new entrants connect earlier in the education process—perhaps mid-point—and thus enable some pre-employment preparation to take place. In the long run, when at long last the world values the skills of information professionals to the point that salaries and career ladders are widely available both within and without the organization, we would see increased numbers of graduates and organizational structures that can accommodate their skills and aspirations.

References

Anderson, D. J. (1985). Comparative career profiles of academic librarians: Are leaders different? *The Journal of Academic Librarianship, 10*(January).

Creth, S. D. (1986). *Effective on-the-job training: Developing library human resources.* Chicago: ALA.

Dailey, C. A. (1982). *Using the track record approach.* New York: AMACOM.

Dewey, B. I. (1987). *Library jobs: How to fill them, how to find them.* Phoenix, AZ: Oryx Press.

Feild, H. S., & Gatewood, R. D. (1987). Matching talent with the task. *Personnel Administrator*, (April), 113-124.

Heim, K. M., & Moen, W. E. (In press). *Occupational entry: Library and information science students' attitudes, demographics and aspirations.* Chicago: ALA.

Heim, K. M. (1988). Librarians for the new millennium. In W. E. Moen & K. M. Heim (Eds.), *Librarians for the new millennium* (pp. 7-9). Chicago: ALA.

Hunt, S. (1983). A structure and seven-step process for developing in-house human resources programs. *The Bookmark, 41*(Summer).

Isacco, J. M., & Smith, C. (1985). Hiring: A common sense approach. *Journal of Library Administration, 6*(2), 67-81.

Phillips, J. J. (1987). *Recruitment, training and retraining new employees.* San Francisco: Jossey-Bass.

Wanous, J. P. (1980). *Organizational entry: Recruitment, selection and socialization of newcomers.* Reading, MA: Addison-Wesley.

JAMES G. NEAL

Assistant Dean and Head
Reference and Instructional Services Division
University Libraries
Pennsylvania State University
University Park, Pennsylvania

Employee Turnover and the Exit Interview

ABSTRACT

Employee turnover is an important measure of the health of an organization. All libraries should implement a three-step program of turnover management: the collection and analysis of data on turnover patterns, the identification of those factors contributing to turnover in the library through organization of a formal exit interview program, and implementation of remedial actions which address the main causes of turnover. This article focuses on the exit interview as an effective tool for documenting the causes of turnover in a library and for influencing management action. The exit interview must be based upon a standardized format, assure employee confidentiality, employ talented interviewing staff, involve periodic assessment of effectiveness, and provide for routine feedback to management.

INTRODUCTION

Libraries, despite a significant dependence on human resources and the substantial costs of personnel replacement, continue to operate without effective employee turnover management programs. Staff turnover—that is, the termination of employees and the hiring of other individuals to replace them—is a complex phenomenon requiring a systematic view and an awareness of many variables within both the work and external environments. Managers in all types and sizes of libraries must expand their understanding of the turnover process and its impact on the employee, the work group, the library, and the larger library community.

EMPLOYEE TURNOVER

Turnover is characterized by two key variables: job satisfaction and opportunity. Job satisfaction, the "push" of internal organizational factors, is the extent to which employees have positive and affective attitudes toward their jobs. Opportunity, the "pull" of the external labor market, is the extent to which alternative occupational roles are available. It is important to distinguish between voluntary and involuntary turnover, as well as avoidable and unavoidable separations. Avoidable separations relate to conditions the employer has some control over such as wages, benefits, and working conditions. Unavoidable separations generally are not controllable by management and include retirement, death and maternity leave. Voluntary turnovers, frequently referred to as quits or resignations, are initiated by the employee while involuntary terminations, such as dismissals or layoffs, are initiated by the employer. Most research on turnover focuses on voluntary and avoidable separations because they are more subject to control by management (Price, 1977).

The focus of management concern is the impact of employee turnover on organizational effectiveness and costs. Turnover can be seen as providing some benefits: helps keep salary costs down, creates opportunities for upward mobility, encourages staffing flexibility and organizational restructuring, brings employees with new ideas and experiences into the organization, and reduces the frustration created by dead-end jobs. The negative consequences tend to be more visible and the costs greater than anticipated. The fiscal impact, sometimes described as the positional replacement costs, can be summarized in several categories: costs incurred when an individual leaves, costs of advertising the position and recruiting and selecting a replacement, costs of new employee orientation and training, costs of equipment underutilization, and costs of lost production and productivity (Flamholtz, 1973).

In view of the significant impact of turnover and the value of turnover as a measure of organizational health, all libraries should implement a three-step program of turnover management: the collection and analysis of data on turnover patterns, the identification of those factors contributing to turnover in the library through organization of a formal exit interview program, and implementation of remedial actions which address the main causes of turnover. This article focuses on the exit interview as an effective tool for documenting the causes of turnover in a library and for influencing management action.

THE EXIT INTERVIEW

The exit interview enables not only an improved understanding of the reasons why employees leave, but provides opportunities for effective communication in several additional areas as well. These include for example: clarification of complaints against employees being released; sharing of information about benefits, including maintenance of medical insurance, pension programs, and eligibility for unemployment compensation; promotion of positive relations with former employees; discussion of policies on references and eligibility for rehire; and identification of problem areas that require corrective measures. The exit interview should not be seen as an opportunity to retain competent employees by exploring the causes of dissatisfaction and seeking solutions to their concerns.

The two major elements of the exit interview are discovery and communication. Neither the discovery of an employee's motivation for vacating a position nor the sharing of this information with management are easy tasks. A commitment of sufficient time and appropriate staff for dialogue, analysis, and feedback is essential. Staff understanding and cooperation are also critical so that the exit interview is viewed as more than another mandatory procedure that must be completed before a final paycheck is issued.

The literature of librarianship provides little information on the use of exit interviews in libraries. A study completed during 1981-82 surveyed the management of 150 North American university libraries on turnover of employees in support staff positions. Findings indicate that approximately 50 percent of these libraries always carried out exit interviews, 36 percent sometimes, and 14 percent never. In addition, the individuals responsible for conducting the exit interviews were identified. In nearly 60 percent of the cases, the library personnel officer or a representative of the university personnel office was involved. The balance of the respondents cited a library administrator or the employee's supervisor as the interviewer, and in three instances it was the preference of the departing employee (Neal, 1982).

Critical to the success of an exit interview program is the structure and content of the contact with the departing employee. Key elements are the clear assignment of responsibility for conducting the interviews, effective scheduling procedures, the creation of a proper climate for the interview, and a productive format. The exit interview does not create a mutually beneficial condition, and, with little to gain from the experience, an employee may be unwilling to provide detailed and accurate information. If the interview is scheduled hastily and conducted haphazardly, it will be even more difficult to identify reasons for termination.

Exit interviews in an organization should be conducted by one individual, preferably a personnel professional who is knowledgeable about the work of the library, who is effective in a private and face-to-face interview setting, and who is trusted by the employees. Credibility and approachability are essential qualities. In some large organizations it may be necessary to share this responsibility by assigning one interviewer to each major employee group. In some small organizations, where a personnel professional is not on the staff, contracting with an outside office or individual may be appropriate.

An important initial question to broach is whether exit interviews will be optional or mandatory. The inclusion of a review of employee benefits and outstanding accounts as part of the interview promotes cooperation and participation. The exit interview should be scheduled in advance and the employee should understand the objectives of the meeting. The literature on exit interviews presents conflicting recommendations on the best timing, some advocating the last day of employment, while others favor a time earlier in the final week. The scheduling of the interview will enable the interviewer to gather information, review appropriate files, discuss relevant issues with the employees' immediate supervisor, and budget sufficient time for the meeting.

The interview should be conducted in a private office in an environment free of interruptions and which encourages an open exchange of information. The interviewer should clearly describe at the outset the format of the meeting, the expectations for the discussions, and the intended use of the information gathered. On this latter point, an employee must be confident that any negative points will not be immediately shared with management and attributed to the employee. Furthermore, because the exit interview is a confidential exchange, information obtained should not be available directly to unemployment compensation claim examiners.

The individual conducting the exit interview should be aware of several basic prejudices the departing employee may bring to the process. The employee may not perceive personal benefits of participation and thus make it difficult for the interviewer to obtain accurate information. A sense of failure or resentment may provoke the employee to exaggerate the difficulties encountered in the organization. If the employee feels that it is either too late or too difficult to effect constructive changes, then it might be viewed as wiser to leave a "clean" and noncontroversial record to avoid problems when applying for other positions.

The format of the exit interview is essential to its success. The interview should have previously defined objectives and subjects for discussion and should be structured and standardized so that generally all employees are asked the same basic questions. The basic purposes of the interview are to draw out the departing employee's opinions about the employment experience and to obtain through discussion an informed understanding of the reasons for termination. In this process, it is essential that the interviewer not introduce personal biases or take a value stand on the accuracy of statements presented.

A basic outline for conducting the exit interview should include the following elements: statement of purpose, relevant background information, positive aspects of the job, negative aspects of the job, critical incidents, reasons for leaving, suggested changes, and separation agreements. Some organizations have found it effective to distribute a pre-interview questionnaire and to use this information as a guide for the interview discussions. Employees may be more willing before the interview to share opinions about the organization, their work, and their supervisors in a written format. The interview itself may be guided by a checklist of areas to be covered including: orientation to the library, on the job training, challenges and opportunities provided by job assignment, participation in broader library and professional activities, major strengths and weaknesses of the department, major strengths and problems of the library from both employee and patron perspectives, major individual contributions to the library, and benefits of employment (University of Michigan Libraries). A series of questions can be developed to serve as the basis for discussions such as:

—What did you like most about your job?
—What did you like least about your job?
—Describe the amount of variety in your job.
—How would you evaluate the quality of the training you received?
—What would you suggest that might improve the orientation/ training of the person who replaces you?
—What could be done to make your job easier/more challenging/more interesting?
—What improvements in communication would make this a better place to work?
—What resources might be made available to make this position better for your successor?
—What contributed to making your employment here enjoyable?
—Do you feel that performance expectations were reasonable and clearly explained?
—Did you receive clear and adequate directions regarding the specific duties of your position?
—How would you characterize the support you got from your supervisor?
—Was the feedback you received about your performance timely, helpful, and specific?
—What makes your new position more attractive than the present job?
—What factors contributed to your decision to leave (University of Indiana)?

Regardless of the structure of the exit interview, it should always include four basic elements: a diagnosis function, a therapy/improvement function, a separation assistance function, and a determination of reasons for leaving function.

THE POST-TURNOVER SURVEY

Many organizations employ a post-turnover survey as a substitute for, or as a complement to, the conventional exit interview. Several advantages are cited for the use of questionnaires. The lapse of time will encourage former employees to make more rational and honest assessments of the employer and supervisor particularly if offering opinions from the security of a new position. If surveys are conducted anonymously, both the employer and the employee are relieved of the pressure of a face-to-face confrontation. The use of questionnaires enables the organization to sample consistently rather than depend on evidence produced by the sporadic statements of individual employees (Yourman, 1965). An effective cover letter can promote participation by stressing the survey objectives as improved employee performance and job satisfaction and by underscoring the anonymity or confidentiality of the responses.

The issue of exit interview versus post-turnover survey comes down to a choice between objectivity of data versus response rate. The effective design of the questionnaire in terms of choice of questions, layout, and language; the ease of completion and minimizing of time commitment; and the identification of the former employee with the objectives of the survey can help to maximize response. Many organizations now rely completely on the survey method and have canceled exit interview programs. Skilled interviewers, able to persuade departing employees to talk honestly about their experiences and decision to leave, are not always available. The unwillingness or inability of personnel managers to follow-up on information received in the interview and to communicate the findings to management compromises the entire process. The questionnaire results similarly should not digress into a record keeping device, for if they do not prompt corrective measures, such surveys quickly become viewed as another futile personnel gimmick.

Benefits and Liabilities of Exit Interviews and Post-Turnover Surveys

Information gathered through exit interviews or surveys is invaluable management data. No exit interview program can proceed successfully without a clear organizational commitment to communicate and act upon the findings. Findings may take the form of aggregate summary reports for senior administrators which document important trends and patterns. This information can be used in departmental/unit reviews, in the identification of areas requiring policy attention, and in the targeting of positions or supervisors experiencing problems. Care must be taken to protect the confidentiality of the employee and to handle discreetly and in a positive manner the feedback of information to individual supervisors.

The exit interview results will generally target several key areas: management practices, employee placement, training and development, compensation and benefits, health and safety, job security, and supervisor/employee relations. Preliminary findings on reasons for turnover in libraries confirm this trend with the following factors most often cited as reasons for leaving (Neal, 1984):

—better opportunities elsewhere

—lack of job challenge
—unfair or unequal treatment
—poor supervision
—weak interpersonal relationships
—unsatisfactory salary
—inability to perform duties effectively
—moving/graduating spouse
—return to school
—inadequate selection/assignment procedures
—ineffective grievance procedures
—lack of well-organized training programs

The key element in the management of employee turnover is exit interview feedback to first line supervisors. They must be informed and knowledgeable about the technical and administrative aspects of their position and about organizational policies and procedures that affect their subordinates. They must be skillful in applying constructive discipline, effective in interpersonal communication, and creative in challenging committed and productive employees. But most importantly, they must understand the positive and negative aspects and impact of their performance as supervisors.

Evaluations of exit interview programs have not been well-documented. Several studies suggest a considerable amount of distortion in the information gathered through exit interviews when compared with the results of surveys completed by the same employees. One study concluded that unavoidable terminations appear to be the only exit interviews that elicit accurate information. This may be due to the unambiguous nature of reasons such as moving or pregnancy. In addition, the extra-organizational nature of such turnover poses little threat when revealed to a management representative during an exit interview (Lefkowitz, 1969). Exit interviews tend to overemphasize the importance of personal reasons and dissatisfaction with work as reasons for terminations, and to underrepresent the desire for freedom of action and autonomy in career planning as well as the attraction of the job market.

With the critical importance of the skills of the interviewer, exit interviews have been consistently criticized for the reliability and validity of the procedure. Furthermore, there is limited data on the extent to which information obtained in interviews has been useful in reducing turnover. In one study, Garretson & Teel (1982) sought to determine whether exit interviews are cost-effective; that is, do savings in turnover costs exceed the costs of the interviews? This investigation reached three major conclusions: for many organizations, the exit interview is a symbolic gesture because no use is made of the information obtained; many organizations are in fact securing information on a variety of factors affecting the quality of work life that could be used as a basis for turnover reduction programs; and little effort is being made to quantify the costs of turnover thus making it impossible to determine whether exit interviews are cost-effective.

The importance of turnover management to organizational effectiveness and success led to a call several years ago for implementation of an action and research agenda on the part of individual libraries and professional organizations (Neal, 1982). These points are still valid. Library managers should begin to collect and analyze data on turnover for their employees and advocate organizationwide turnover monitoring programs. Procedures should be organized—preferably well-designed exit interviews—to identify those factors which are contributing to turnover problems in the library and remedial programs should be implemented which address these problems. Professional organizations must take a leadership position in the promotion of turnover management in libraries. The formulation of guidelines for the collection, measurement, and reporting of turnover data would enable and encourage the computation of benchmark statistics for groups of employees in libraries, for different size institutions, and for geographic regions. The profession must also promote substantive research on turnover-related topics including analysis of turnover trends in individual or groups of libraries and testing of the assorted variables related to turnover in library settings.

The exit interview is thus a central component of effective turnover management. By allowing an employee to obtain closure of employment with an organization, the exit interview provides for the establishment of good working relations with former employees, and furnishes useful management data. It must be based upon a standardized format, assure employee confidentiality, employ talented interviewing staff, involve periodic assessment of effectiveness, and provide for routine feedback to management.

REFERENCES

Flamholtz, E. G. (1973). Human resources accounting: Measuring positional replacement costs. *Human Resource Management, 12*(Spring), 8-16.

Indiana University. Exit Interview University checklist from Indiana University Libraries.

Garretson, P., & Teel, K. S. (1982). The exit interview: Effective tool or meaningless gesture? *Personnel, 59*(July/August), 70-77.

Lefkowitz, J., & Katz, M. L. (1969). Validity of exit interviews. *Personnel Psychology, 22*(Winter), 445-455.

Neal, J. G. (1984). The turnover process and the academic library. In G. B. McCabe & B. Kreissman (Eds.), *Advances in Library Administration and Organization* (Vol. 3). Greenwich, CT: JAI Press.

Neal, J. G. (1982). Staff turnover and the academic library. In G. B. McCabe & B. Kreissman (Eds.), *Foundations in library and information science. (Options for the 80s: Proceedings of the second national conference of the Association of College and Research Libraries)* (Vol. 17, Part A) (pp. 99-106). Greenwich, CT: JAI Press.

Price, J. L. (1977). *The study of turnover.* Ames, IA: Iowa State University Press.

University of Michigan. Exit interview form from University of Michigan Libraries.

Yourman, J. (1965). Following up on terminations: An alternative to the exit interview. *Personnel, 42*(July/August), 51-55.

LUCY R. COHEN

Manager
Personnel and Payroll Services
University of Michigan Library
Ann Arbor, Michigan

Conducting Performance Evaluations

Abstract

In order for any performance evaluation system to be effective, it should provide believable information about a staff member's job performance. A performance evaluation system based on performance goals and measures is an effective system which satisfies those conditions. This article provides a summary of the discussions and materials covered during the performance evaluation workshop conducted at the 29th Allerton Institute. It reviews the reasons for conducting performance evaluations, the concerns and potential pitfalls to performance evaluations, and provides an in-depth description of a goals-based performance evaluation system.

Introduction

Any effective performance evaluation system should provide believable information about a staff member's job performance. A staff member's performance evaluation should not be based on personal traits nor should it be subject to the rater's bias. It should be based on reliable, valid, and comparative data on job performance (Winstansley, 1980). A performance evaluation system based on performance goals and measures is an effective system which satisfies those conditions. In addition, this type of system also provides ample opportunities for developing staff members, communicating expectations, and coaching them in areas of performance deficiency.

The performance evaluation workshop this author conducted at this Allerton Institute on *Critical Issues in Library Personnel Management,* provided an opportunity to discuss reasons why supervisors and managers should conduct performance evaluations as well as concerns or problems associated with performance evaluations. It also provided an opportunity to be introduced to the goals-based performance evaluation system and to practice writing performance goals. The following provides a summary of the discussions and the materials covered during the workshop.

REASONS FOR CONDUCTING PERFORMANCE EVALUATIONS

Participants agreed that performance evaluations were necessary to provide documentation for personnel actions including merit increases, promotions, and disciplinary action. In addition, it was generally agreed that the evaluations afforded an opportunity for the supervisor to provide a written record of a staff member's overall job performance. The participants also agreed that performance evaluations were developmental in nature since they provided supervisors an opportunity to note performance deficiencies and other areas of concern. Participants noted that supervisors could use performance evaluation information as a planning tool for determining what additional staff training is needed.

An additional important aspect of performance evaluation identified was better communication between the supervisor and the staff member.

CONCERNS ABOUT PERFORMANCE EVALUATIONS

Some participants stated that they wanted the performance evaluation to be a positive experience for both the supervisor and the staff member. Some were concerned about the time it takes to do performance evaluations, others about getting a commitment from supervisors not only to do them, but also to do them honestly and in a timely manner.

Merits of pay for performance were discussed by participants with some concerned that there was no monetary incentive for union employees, others were concerned about how to implement bonus plans linked to goals, yet others wanted to separate developmental performance evaluations from ones linked to pay increases. Participants agreed that an additional concern was obtaining objective data on which to base performance evaluations and to ensure consistency in rating staff members' performance.

POTENTIAL PITFALLS TO PERFORMANCE EVALUATION

Before introducing the goals-based system, the following potential pitfalls to performance evaluation were reviewed and adapted from "8 Ways to Ruin Performance Review" (Lowe, 1986).

1. *Halo Effect*—the supervisor gives a favorable rating to all position responsibilities based on impressive performance in one job function.
2. *Pitchfork Effect*—the opposite of the "halo effect," the supervisor

gives a poor rating to all position responsibilities based on poor performance in one job function.

3. *Central Tendency*—the supervisor rates everyone as average, thereby avoiding making judgments.
4. *Loose Rater*—the supervisor rates everyone highly (this type of rater can also be called spineless or lenient). The supervisor thus avoids conflict by not pointing out weaknesses.
5. *Tight Rater*—the supervisor rates everyone poorly because he feels no one can live up to his standards.
6. *Recency Error*—the supervisor relies on recent events to determine a staff member's performance rating rather than the full period under review.
7. *Length of Service Bias*—the supervisor assumes that a tenured staff member is performing well because of his experience.
8. *Competitive Rater*—the supervisor determines a staff member's rating based on how he has been evaluated by his own supervisor.

THE GOALS-BASED PERFORMANCE EVALUATION SYSTEM

Participants were introduced to the goals-based system (Creth, 1984) by reviewing the 10 step process. The flow chart (see Fig. 1) illustrates the goals-based performance evaluation process—i.e., performance planning, monitoring, and evaluation. The activities shown above the shaded areas are those designated for the supervisor; activities within the shaded area are for the employee. The activities in the center are shared jointly by the supervisor and the employee.

The main objective of this performance evaluation system is to establish communication between the supervisor and employee in areas of responsibility, desired results and outcomes, priorities, development, and evaluation of work performed.

PERFORMANCE PLANNING

Major Areas of Responsibilities Agreement
The first step in the process of performance planning is to update the job description. This provides an opportunity to define the responsibilities of a staff member. The areas of responsibilities agreement should also include new directions and projects which are inherent in organizational change (i.e., how the unit and divisional goals and plans will affect the employee).

Performance Plan and Developing Performance Goals
There are several methods to develop a performance plan. One way is to delegate the responsibility to the employee and then have the plan validated by the supervisor. Another way is to have the supervisor and employee work out a plan individually and then meet to review and jointly agree on the goals. The latter is suggested in order to allow the

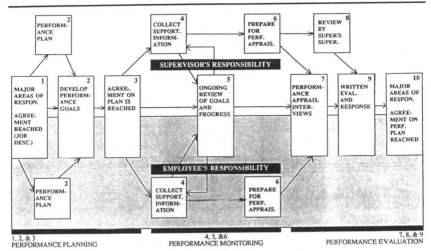

*Adapted from the University of Michigan Hospital Performance Evaluation Program
Prepared by Lucy R. Cohen, University Library, University of Michigan, 1987

Figure 1. Flow chart of an evaluation system based on performance goals*

supervisor an opportunity to participate fully and use this process as a
tool for planning unit work and priorities. In addition, this process
provides the supervisor the opportunity to assist in developing action
plans for areas of problem performance. Supervisors should:
—review broader unit/divisional goals and how the employee can
  contribute;
—review the past performance of an employee in order to identify and
  consider areas of strength and weakness;
—provide assistance in articulating goals for improving areas of
  weakness.
Employees should:
—outline major continuing responsibilities and desired results;
—write goals for projects, new programs, improvements, and professional development;
—review goals to ensure that they are: measurable; support unit/
  divisional goals and activities, realistic, and under the employee's
  control and within the employee's own areas of responsibility.

Agreement on a Plan is Reached
    It is important to arrive at a mutual understanding on all areas of
responsibility, performance goals, and methods for measuring results.
If differences in opinions, priorities, or perspectives exist, these must be
resolved prior to agreement on the goals.

PERFORMANCE MONITORING

Collect Supportive Information
    Data collection should occur throughout the period under review.

Supportive information which directly relates to the performance objectives and the measurement criteria (indicators and standards) for each performance goal should be collected by both the supervisor and the employee. Supervisors and employees should:
—review personal notes and observations and feedback received from others;
—review external factors or obstacles which prohibit achievement of desired outcomes; and
—review any alterations in unit/divisional priorities and any other changes that have occurred over the period under review.

Ongoing Review of Goals and Progress
Another major objective of a goals-based performance evaluation system is to provide timely feedback to the employee. To make this system work, it is imperative that these opportunities occur frequently, no fewer than quarterly for an annual goals-setting cycle. Supervisors and employees should:
—review progress on goals;
—adjust, modify, add, or drop goals;
—adjust priorities due to changes in organizational directions; and
—review expectations and responsibilities.
Supervisors should:
—provide assistance in identifying areas that need improvement;
—provide recognition of accomplishments and contributions;
—focus on job performance;
—assist in articulating action plans for problem areas of performance;
—provide a coaching framework.
Note that the previous steps regarding the collection of supportive information and the ongoing review of goals and progress should be repeated regularly throughout the performance evaluation cycle.

Prepare for Performance Appraisal
Prior to the formal performance appraisal interview and the written evaluation which occurs at the end of an agreed upon time period (usually on an annual basis), the supervisor and employee need to prepare by reviewing the collective supportive information and the employee's performance in relation to agreed upon goals and stands.

PERFORMANCE EVALUATION
Performance Appraisal Interview
This interview is mutual working session. A date and time for the interview should be set in advance and held in a private location. Sufficient time should be allocated to conduct the interview without interruption or rushing. Supervisors and employees should:
—discuss employee's activities in order to arrive at an understanding of achievements and problems;

—review each performance goal, the desired outcome of the goal (results), and assess what did or did not occur;

—discuss accomplishments on specific goals;

—discuss problems and what prevented the employee from producing the required results; what obstacles were impeding progress and job satisfaction;

—discuss ways the supervisor can be more helpful in the coming year; and

—discuss performance goals for the next year and a time frame for preparing the performance plan.

Review by Supervisor's Superior

An opportunity to discuss the appraisal with the supervisor's superior (manager) is important for several reasons: the manager can often provide additional information on the employee's performance as well as provide the broader view of the organization for future planning; the manager can provide additional information on the possibilities for training and advancement for the employee; and the supervisor's work with the employee is reviewed as part of his own performance plan with the manager.

Written Evaluation and Response

The written evaluation provides the opportunity to document the employee's performance during the past year. This evaluation becomes a part of the employee's permanent file. Supervisors should:

—provide a balanced and clear statement that reflects accurately the performance appraisal interview;

—provide data and cite specific results achieved in addressing performance goals;

—summarize strengths and performance areas which need improvement or development, and provide examples to support appraisal;

—describe areas for which new goals need to be written or previous goals revised.

Employees should:

—respond formally to the evaluation, commenting on their own perceptions. Sign the evaluation, thereby validating they have read the review.

Areas of Responsibilities/Performance Plan Agreement

The cycle begins again with an agreement on areas of responsibility and a new performance plan. Performance goals and criteria for measuring these goals are agreed upon once more.

After discussing the process of formulating performance goals, the rest of the workshop consisted of defining the four types of performance goals (see Appendix A), reviewing sample goals (see Appendix B), and practicing the writing of performance goals.

Before participants had an opportunity to practice writing performance goals, it was important to review that it is the *process* of writing goals that is more important than the goal itself. The process of writing goals forces the staff member or the supervisor to identify the expected outcome and the desired results. It allows for a staff member or supervisor to begin formulating performance standards, performance measures, and action plans. When attempting to formulate performance goals, the staff member or supervisor should try to answer the following questions: What needs to get done? (What are the expected outcomes and the anticipated results?) What is good enough? (What is the standard?) How will we know? (What are the performance indicators and what is going to be measured?)

At the end of the workshop the participants attempted to formulate personal performance goals or performance goals for their staff. These first attempts were shared in small and large groups. The additional references to the article provide an opportunity to further investigate this topic.

APPENDIX A

Definitions

PERFORMANCE GOALS

Performance goals are written definitions of what you expect to accomplish within a given time period. Goals may relate to continuous job responsibilities, to specific one-time projects, to implementation of new services or operations, to plans for improvement of service or production, to learning a new job or developing a new skill. Some types of goals will be applicable every year; some will not. For each planning year, however, goals should encompass all major job responsibilities, all significant investments of time and energy, and all plans that require special allocation of time, funds, or personnel. Most goal statements will include desired result, performance indicators, and standards. Some goal statements will be accompanied by an action plan.

PERFORMANCE INDICATORS AND STANDARDS

Indicators describe *what* is to be used as a measure of performance. Standards define the expected *level* of achievement. Measures of performance may be difficult to establish. They are often easier to define for jobs that are production oriented and for tasks where results can be described in terms of quantity, elapsed time, or accuracy. It is more difficult to set standards for providing services when the product is information or advice, the value of which varies according to the recipient—such as reference service, staff counseling, or consulting. You may not be satisfied with your first attempt at identifying indicators and standards, but you should describe as well as you can how the accomplishment of each goal can be measured or evaluated.

ACTION PLAN

An action plan outlines the steps to be taken to accomplish a goal, sets time limits for accomplishing each step, and establishes an expected completion date. It describes a series of activities that will result in the achievement of a performance goal. Action plans should accompany all problem-solving goals, innovative goals, and development goals—any goal that involves a limited time frame and a final result. Goals relating to routine ongoing job responsibilities will not necessarily be accompanied by an action plan. At the time you are preparing your annual performance goals, you may know that you intend to carry out a particular project, but at that point may have only an indefinite idea of the steps required to accomplish it. In this case, you can simply indicate that a more complete action plan will be prepared by a certain date. The details can be written later.

TYPES OF GOALS

Although not all goals will fall neatly into a category, most can be identified as belonging to one of the following general types: maintenance, problem-solving, innovative, or developmental.

Maintenance Goals

Maintenance goals are the major substance of your work and are the goals by which performance is most heavily judged. They should cover all primary ongoing job responsibilities and should, therefore, be related to your job description. These goals are likely to remain stable every year. The level of detail

APPENDIX A *(Cont.)*

Definitions

described by goal statements may differ according to job complexity and personal preference in stating them, but each primary responsibility should stand as a separate goal. Whenever possible, goals should be stated in terms of the desired result, not as an activity.

Problem-Solving Goals

Problem-solving goals often relate to continuing responsibilities. They may solve a specific problem or address a need to bring productivity or quality of service up to an established standard. You may have a goal to raise previously set standards or even to establish a standard for the first time. What was a maintenance goal last year may this year become a problem-solving goal. If the desired result is achieved, this same goal will revert to a maintenance goal again next year. Problem-solving goals should be accompanied by an action plan.

Innovative Goals

Innovative goals are new plans, innovations, onetime efforts that require special planning. They may be undertaken for various reasons—to respond to changed users' needs, to take advantage of new technology, or to expand services. They often provide opportunities to be creative. Innovative goals should be challenging, should stretch the individual, and should produce a significant result for the library. They should have a purpose, which should be included in the goal statement. Innovative goals especially need careful planning. Attention must be given to what resources will be required, what the costs will be, how long it will take, who will be involved, and what checkpoints along the way will be used to measure progress.

Performance on innovative goals is measured by the degree of success in completing on schedule the steps of an organized action plan and in achieving the desired result. However, the nature of the goals you set for yourself may be as important in the evaluation of performance as whether or not an individual goal is achieved. For example, the accomplishment of a plan to make a minor procedural change in unit operations may not be viewed as being of equal importance as a major innovation in the organization of the unit, even if unavoidable circumstances prevented completion of the latter by the projected date.

Developmental Goals

Developmental goals apply to an individual learning a new job or developing a new skill that will improve job performance. These goals, like problem-solving and innovative goals, should include action plans describing the steps to be taken, target dates, and levels of performance to be achieved.

Professional Contributions

You should also include goal statements covering major committee or other university library assignments that require a significant commitment of time. Appointments to university committees, task forces, or other bodies that make demands on time or resources should be included as well. A brief descriptive statement should be adequate. Unless you are the chairperson, you will rarely have sufficient information to include an action plan. Professional commitments outside the university should, with rare exception, only be reported at the end of the year as documentation in support of promotion.

By permission, condensed from: Creth, S. (1984). *Performance evaluation: A goals-based approach*. Association of College and Research Libraries. Continuing Education Program #106.

Appendix B

Sample Performance Goals

Maintenance Goals

Goal: Smooth workflow in section resulting in no backlog of work in one area causing insufficient or uneven workload in another area and maintenance of an average processing time of one week for all rush materials.

Goal: Trash is removed daily, and furniture is damp wiped. Carpeted floor vacuumed weekly, other areas wet mopped. Bathrooms are cleaned and materials are replaced daily. Unusual cleaning needs are noted and completed.

Performance Indicators: 10 percent error rate for routine duties (trash removal, vacuuming and dusting and 0 error rate in priority areas such as bathrooms). (Job description: clean designated areas of 6 west)

Problem-Solving Goals

Goal: Achieve an approval plan profile that results in a return of 10 percent or less materials received and acquisition of 90 percent or more of appropriate titles in order to increase the efficiency of the approval program.

Action Plan:
1. Meet with vendor representative to discuss current profile—December 1985.
2. Review books received for the following four months for relevance.
3. Revise profile as needed—April 1986.
4. Review receipts against comprehensive checklists for coverage by approval plan.
5. Modify profile as needed to achieve maximum return rate of 10 percent and minimum acquisition rate of 90 percent—July 1986.

Goal: New staff are able to work independently at established performance levels within six weeks of hire.

Action Plan:
1. Review job requirements and determine areas for which training must be provided on the job.
2. Identify objectives for training for specific tasks for a specific estimated time.
3. Identify staff with whom new employees must meet to review department activities or to receive specific instruction.
4. Identify materials and resources needed for the training process.
5. Review basic training plan in relation to new employee's skills and experience.
6. Develop written training plan and schedule before a person's first day of work.

Innovative Goal

Goal: Have an online acquisition system with fund account capability in place by May 1986 in order to consolidate the ordering and payment processes for monographs and serials and to provide adequate audit trails for university auditors and fund management reports for selectors and library administrators.

Action Plan:
1. Establish objectives—September 1985
2. Review needs of selectors, administrators, auditor and acquisitions staff— September 1985
3. Identify viable systems and schedule site visits or vendor visits working with AD for Technical Services and Head, Serials Division—October 1985

4. Review the systems' capabilities and gather any further information necessary from vendors—November 1985
5. Present a report to library administration identifying preferred system and justifying its selection over other systems—December 1985
6. Assist administration in preparing contracts and other documents necessary for purchase—December '85/January '86
7. Begin to plan implementation—March 1986, etc....

REFERENCES

Creth, S. D. (1984). *Performance evaluation: A goals-based approach*. Chicago, IL: The Association for College & Research Libraries (Continuing Education Program #106).

Lowe, T. R. (1986). Eight ways to ruin performance review. *Personnel Journal, 65*(1986), 60-62.

Winstansley, N. B. (1980). Legal and ethical issues in performance appraisals. *Harvard Business Review, 58*(6), 186-188, 192.

ADDITIONAL REFERENCES

Allan, A., & Reynolds, K. J. (1983). Performance problems: A model for analysis and resolution. *The Journal of Academic Librarianship, 9*(May), 83-88.

Diffie-Couch, P. (1983). How to give feedback. *Supervisory Management, 28*(August), 27-31.

Evans, E. G., & Rugass, B. (1983). Another look at performance appraisal in libraries. *Journal of Library Administration, 3*(Summer), 61-69.

Graves, P. J. (1982). Let's Put Appraisal Back in Performance Appraisal: Part I. *Personnel Journal, 61*(11), 844-849.

Graves, P. J. (1982). Let's Put Appraisal Back in Performance Appraisal: Part II. *Personnel Journal, 61*(12), 918-923.

Hodge, S. P. (1983). Performance appraisals: Developing a sound legal and managerial system. *College and Research Libraries, 44*(July), 235-244.

Kroll, H. R. (1983). Beyond evaluation: Performance appraisal as a planning and motivational tool in libraries. *Journal of Academic Librarianship, 9*(March), 27-32.

SHARON L. BAKER

Assistant Professor
School of Library and
Information Science
University of Iowa
Iowa City, Iowa

Managing Resistance to Change

ABSTRACT

While some resistance to change is inevitable, this article suggests that inept management strategies can often cause the normal unease asso ciated with a change to accelerate into more severe problems. Reasons for negative reactions to change are explored and practical solutions, based on findings of research studies, are offered.

INTRODUCTION

One of the best recent articles on the subject of change was published in 1986 by Sara Fine. One of Fine's most relevant points is that resistance to change is inevitable, and management must be prepared to respond to it (Fine, 1986).

Fine's research shows that "human beings tend to resist change, even when change represents growth and development...[and will lead to] greater efficiency and productivity. [Since] changes in an organization affect the individuals within that organization, and individuals...have the power to facilitate or thwart the implementation of an innovation (Fine, 1986, p. 84).

Why do employees resist change? Primarily because they fear the unknown. That is, they feel anxiety about how the change will affect them, their job performance, their relationship with other employees, and other job related factors. In fact, psychologists say that fear of the unknown is a rational, rather than an irrational, response to change. A small amount of uneasiness is to be expected from most people when the status quo shifts, simply because people need time to adjust their

53

thinking, their job performance, and their social relationships to any changes made.

Thus, resistance to change is inevitable, and managers must allow for some resistance when they are planning to implement change. Indeed, some resistance to change may even be positive because it slows down the speed with which innovation might otherwise proceed and allows time for people to adjust to it (Fine, 1986, pp. 88-89).

Unfortunately, resistance to change sometimes goes beyond a healthy unease for the unknown, as some researchers have discovered. Nancy Feldman (1972) studied a series of changes in the Tulsa Public Library system and found the following types of employee resistance: task avoidance or postponement, hostility (stated or unstated), resignation, and underproduction (meeting only the minimum expectations of one's work). A few years later, other library researchers found several more indicators of employee resistance to change: increased absenteeism, increased employee impatience, frustration, and sabotage (Plate & Stone, 1974; Veaner, 1974).

To manage change effectively, administrators must understand why an employee's initial reaction to a new proposal, that is, uneasiness and fear of the unknown, sometimes accelerates into more negative behavior like decreased job performance or sabotage.

What Causes Negative Behavior in Employees

Fine (1986) implies that a major cause of this acceleration is inept management (pp. 91-92). This article will, therefore, explore two questions: Can managers actually increase employee levels of resistance to change through poor planning, lack of support, or ignorance of employee needs? And, if so, how can managers avoid doing this in the future?

General Uncertainty about the Effects of Change

Let us scrutinize the general uncertainty which people experience when a major change is announced by a hypothetical example. Upper managers in an academic library are concerned because employees do not have enough time to evaluate the library's collection. These managers are quite altruistic; they want to try to make their employees' jobs easier by bringing in a consultant to conduct the evaluation for them.

Sherry, the head of collection development, is asked to make this a top priority. Since she has not worked out all the details of who the consultant will be and what he will do, she makes a simple bald statement at the end of her next staff meeting. The statement is this: a consultant will be brought in to evaluate the library's collection, review collection development policies, and make suggestions for improving collection development efforts. Sherry does not encourage discussion about the matter because the meeting has already run over in time. When staff try to briefly question the need, she says upper management has asked her to implement this change and that she will try to answer people's questions later.

George is one of sixteen employees responsible for collection development at this library. He has a number of immediate reactions to the suggested change—that is, to the consultant's presence. He wants to know who the consultant will be and what is the consultant's level of expertise. He wants to know why management feels a consultant is necessary (e.g., does management feel the current collection development staff is doing a bad job?). He also wants to know whether the consultant will discuss matters fully with current staff before making decisions which will affect them and how any changes suggested will affect patron service in the long run.

George's boss, Sherry, is too busy with her normal work and with making arrangements for the consultant's visit to answer his questions. George's initial reaction to the announcement is uneasiness, but as Sherry continues to ignore his needs for more complete information on the topic, he begins to feel that she is hiding something from him. His anxiety about the consultant's presence grows. By the time the consultant arrives, George's stress about the situation has grown so much that he is unwilling to listen to any of the consultant's suggestions. Instead he tries to undermine the consultant's advice by disagreeing with everything.

In this case, Sherry has handled the introduction of the new change poorly. She has failed to see the extent of George's uneasiness about this change and to provide him and other employees with appropriate information to ease these fears.

The literature of librarianship, of management, and of personnel psychology shows that employees respond better to change when management consciously tries to ease employee fears in a number of ways (Werbel, 1983; Weinbach, 1986; Malinconico, 1983).

First, management should provide as much advance information about the actual change as possible. Sherry did not. She hadn't worked out all the details herself and may have been afraid of looking inept in front of her staff if she said this. But she should have provided as much information as possible and not worried about the details at this point.

Second, management should fully inform affected employees of the reasons behind the change. In the case mentioned, management is trying to help employees by providing a person to perform a task which they have not had time to do. Since this rationale is not made clear, George assumes management is criticizing the ability of the staff to evaluate the collection and reacts accordingly.

Third, management should do everything possible to clarify employees' questions about the changes. Sherry did not realize how serious George's uneasiness about the change was. Thus she did not take the time to answer his questions, unwittingly making the situation worse.

Fourth, management should give employees time to reflect on how the proposed change will affect them, the organization as a whole, and their clientele. Sherry, told by upper management that bringing in the consultant is a top priority, rushes to do this rather than discussing matters fully with her staff and trying to give them time to adjust to the change.

In other words, workers who receive clear information about how a change will directly affect the organization and their role within it will accept change significantly better than those who do not receive this information.

A second example might make this even clearer. A 1985 article by two communications researchers described the results of a study of a government agency which was anticipating a move to a new office building (Miller, 1985). The employees had always worked in traditional offices, but management was asking them to move to a new building which used open landscaping. The move represented an environmental shift which could radically alter processes for accomplishing work (Miller, 1985, p. 371). Six weeks before the move, management had provided little information to the employees about the change even though it had been planned for some time.

The researchers asked senior management at this agency if they could experiment with the levels of information employees got about the move. In effect, the researchers wanted to verify the fact that giving employees clear information in advance would help them adapt better to the change. But the researchers had a second purpose too. They wanted to see whether employees would respond differently if they were given positive information about the move than if they were given negative information.

They did this by emphasizing for one set of departments positive aspects of the move (e.g., more up-to-date furniture and equipment). For another set, they emphasized negative aspects (e.g., the lack of privacy in the open environment). They gave no information to a third set.

The researchers expected to find that employees would adapt to change better when they received positive information about the change and they did. However, employees who had received negative information about the move responded more positively than employees who had received no clarifying information at all. That is, workers who received clarifying information about a change accepted it significantly better than those who did not *even when they viewed the change as a negative one.*

These findings clearly reinforce the idea that managers should share as much information about a proposed change as they can, even if there are negative aspects. That is, when the director of a small medical library is told his budget will be cut by 15 percent next year, he should not try to keep the information under cover. Rather, he should share the news with the staff and then work to keep them informed of and involved about what changs will have to be made to stay within the budget and how these changes will affect them individually.

Uncertainty about Job Performance

Another reason for employee fear of change is uncertainty about new work-related expectations associated with job performance. Specifically, the employee fears that he may not have enough skill to perform the changed task.

A recent study supports this by showing that individuals with experience performing a specific task one way will resist change more than individuals with less experience (Sagie et al., 1985). This was discovered in an experiment where two groups of high school students were asked to complete a series of simple manual tasks where they were rewarded for correct performance. One group was given more experience than the other, and developed more skill at the tasks. They were then asked to adopt automated procedures for these tasks. The students with more experience resisted automation significantly more than those with less experience. This was because the experienced group of workers had a higher degree of confidence in their ability to do the job in the old (i.e., manual) way; when they were asked to automate, their initial anxiety was higher. The levels of uncertainty about performance for students with little experience in their jobs did not change when they were asked to automate. This was because they were still a bit unsure about their performance in the manual task and were thus more receptive to trying new work methods.

This research implies that managers need to follow two strategies when introducing new tasks. First, they need to provide employees with exact information about what the changed tasks will be because knowledge reduces fear. Second, managers need to reassure their employees that they will develop the skills to do these tasks. The latter can be accomplished if workers receive adequate and complete training and receive reassurance that they will not be punished if their performance levels drop initially while relearning the changed tasks.

Employee Participation in Change

Management can also lessen resistance to change by increasing employee involvement in the change process. Henry Lucas lists some of the strengths of encouraging employee participation in change. First, participation increases employee knowledge about the innovation thus lessening fear. Second, participation can be ego enhancing, intrinsically satisfying, and challenging, thus making workers feel needed and appreciated. Finally, participation encourages employees to believe that they have some control over a system that will affect them (Lucas, 1974, pp. 49). This last point is particularly important since psychologists have shown that even small amounts of individual control over adverse stimuli will reduce a person's opposition to these stimuli (Gratchel & Proctor, 1976).

A recent article by Debra Shaw (1986) also supports the idea that participation can reduce resistance to change. In 1983 the Indiana State Library surveyed employees to determine their initial feelings about installing an automated catalog and circulation system. Management then attempted to involve as many staff as possible in planning for the automated system.

Participation was encouraged through a library automation planning committee and through a committee which concentrated on staff development for automation. Each committee was comprised of senior management and volunteers. Both committees shared information about their tasks with various library departments and invited suggestions from the departments for consideration. Several other techniques were also used to keep staff involved and informed, ranging from a regular news memo to programs which acquainted staff with automation terminology and with various automated systems. One year after the study began, staff attitudes were significantly more positive about the proposed new system.

Two cautions need to be offered about participative management. Token participation for employees is not enough. Participative management will only ease resistance to innovation when employees truly believe they can influence the change. In fact, Wilson Luquire (1976) found that attitudes relating to innovation (which in this case was the introduction of OCLC in academic libraries) were directly related to the real level of participative management in the libraries (p. 48). Real level refers to the level to which employees were actually allowed to influence decisions rather than the level to which managers said employees were allowed to influence decisions.

A second caution is also in order. Not all staff members are interested in participatory management. The Indiana State Library appropriately encouraged involvement by volunteers. This approach may be the wisest if a number of people are not interested in participating in the decision-making process.

Fear of Change Due to Social Consequence

One other major type of employee fear is caused when the potential social consequences of the change are not anticipated and allowed for. Perhaps this is best illustrated when looking at the effects of hiring a new director in a fairly small public library. Let's say that the old director had been at the library for twenty years and is retiring. The ten employees have been trained by, and have worked well with, the old director. In this situation each of the employees is not only nervous about whether the new director will be satisfied with their individual performance, but also they are nervous about how the new director will relate to them both as a person and as an employee. In other words, they are nervous that the change might have unanticipated (and negative) social consequences.

In fact, the levels of employee stress just after the hiring of a new director tend to be very high. One main way the new director can reduce stress levels is to be very careful during his first few months on the job to treat employees as if he likes each and every one of them and as if he recognizes the unique contributions that each is offering the library.

Resistance because of Failure to Prove Change is Needed

Resistance to change also occurs when managers fail to convince employees that the change is needed. In one public library in Ohio, library staff resisted efforts to reintegrate the genre fiction collection into the general fiction collection. Management wanted to do this because they felt one interfiled system would make it easier for the technical services staff to inventory the collection since they wouldn't have to look in three or four possible places for a particular book. However, the staff noted that patrons liked having mysteries and other genre areas separated out from the regular collection and that inventories were conducted only once every ten years. In this case, the employees perceived that the proposed change was not a valid one. Ultimately management agreed to let the collection remain separate by genre.

Change should only be implemented when a performance gap exists—that is, when people become highly dissatisfied with some aspect of a task or process. Remember the study of high school students performing the simple manual tasks. The experienced group was finally persuaded to change by an astute manager who made them consider the performance gap, showing them that automation would enable them to complete the work in a fraction of the time (Sagie et al., 1985, p. 160).

The implication here is that management must do a good job identifying and publicizing areas where true performance gaps exist if they expect employees to feel that they have valid reasons for changing. It also implies that if a performance gap does not really exist, management should reconsider the change.

Failure to Commit Sufficient Resources to the Change

Increased resistance to change can also result when managers do not follow through by committing sufficient resources to the change. In one public library, initial employee reactions to the introduction of an automated circulation system and online catalog were generally positive. However, upper management failed to hire an expert to introduce automation, skimped on system specifications, purchased an inferior automated system, and overworked existing personnel to get the system started. Several years later, the automated circulation system was down as much as it was up, required an average twenty second response time when it was up, and had increased both employee and patron dissatisfaction with the library. In addition, machine-readable information on the library's collection had to be input twice since system failures caused much of the data to be erroneously erased from the computer's memory banks. The staff who were initially supportive of the system developed higher and higher levels of frustration and eventually turned against the system. This is clearly a case where administrators failed to commit sufficient resources to planning and implementing a large change and directly increased employee resistance.

Actually, Fine (1986, p. 92) suggests that it is not uncommon for resources (particularly personnel resources) to be overextended or withdrawn just when staff is experiencing the greatest stress of change. Moreover, she adds that administrators often skimp on really necessary items, e.g., complete training by experts may be viewed as an extravagance rather than as a necessary expenditure associated with change. Thus, it is important for managers to be particularly sensitive to this issue, and to critically examine if they have supported the innovation by providing all necessary resources—be it money, time, increased attention to detail by management, added personnel, or whatever.

Resistance Due to Failure to Tie Library Values to the Change
Another reason that employees resist change is that management often forgets to emphasize the positive aspects of the change on professional and library values—e.g., improved service to patrons. Unfortunately, some managers fail both to keep employees informed of the library's values (which should be revealed through the library's statements of its mission and goals), and then to tie the positive effects of the change to these values. Remember George, the worker who resisted efforts to hire a consultant to evaluate the collection. He might have responded more appropriately if management had tied the positive effects of the change to a goal which he supported—i.e., matching collections to patron needs. In other words, if managers insist on hiring a collection evaluation consultant, they need to explain that they are doing this to make sure that collection development efforts are really meeting user needs.

Resistance Due to Failure to Create a Climate Conducive to Change
General resistance to change may also result when managers fail to create a positive climate where change can flourish. The best illustration of this might be a library where management allows employees little participation and in fact does not encourage new ideas in any way. Research has shown that employees resist change less when they are given opportunities to participate in continuing education activities, in professional organization activities, and in professional training—e.g., the MLS degree (Maag, 1975). Each of these activities encourages employees to think and to act for themselves. The activities both expose workers to new ideas and give them confidence in their abilities to respond to new situations. Therefore, workers become more receptive to

changes which are proposed and shown to be valid. This implies that managers need to both encourage and reward employee efforts to learn and grow as this will reinforce receptivity to change.

SUMMARY

Fine (1986) originally implied that inept management strategies can cause resistance to change to accelerate. Both logic and research support this statement and show us the need for corrective management action. Corrective action can include providing adequate information about change and being generally sensitive to employee fears about change. Other positive steps include convincing employees that a real reason exists for the change and committing sufficient resources to the change to ease the transition process and alleviate employee frustration. Managers should also tie the change to improved patron service and should constantly work to create a climate where employees are encouraged to explore new ideas and try them out.

REFERENCES

Feldman, N. G. (1972). Pride in heritage—or resentment?: A sociologist analyzes library staff reaction. *Wilson Library Bulletin, 46*(January), 436-40.
Fine, S. F. (1986). Technological innovation, diffusion and resistance: A historical perspective. *Journal of Library Administration, 7*(Spring), 83-108.
Gratchel, R. J., & Proctor, J. D. (1976). Physiological correlates of learned helplessness in man. *Journal of Abnormal Psychology, 85*(February), 27-34.
Lucas, H. C., Jr. (1974). *Toward creative system design.* New York: Columbia University Press.
Luquire, W. (1976). *Selected factors affecting library staff perceptions of an innovative system: A study of ARL libraries on OCLC.* Ph.D. dissertation, Indiana University.
Maag, A. F. (1975). *Some correlates of program change in large academic libraries.* Ph.D. dissertation. Ohio State University.
Malinconico, S. M. (1983). Listening to the resistance. *Library Journal, 108*(February 15), 353-55.
Miller, K. I., & Monge, P. R. (1985). Social information and employee anxiety about organizational change. *Human Communication Research, 11*(Spring), 365-386.
Plate, K. H., & Stone, E. W. (1974). Factors affecting librarians job satisfaction: A report of two studies. *Library Quarterly, 44*(April), 97-110.
Sagie, A., et al. (1985). Job experience, persuasion strategy and resistance to change: An experimental study. *Journal of Occupational Behavior, 6*(April), 157-162.
Shaw, D. (1986). Staff opinions in library automation planning. *Special Libraries, 77*(Summer), 140-151.
Veaner, A. B. (1974). Institutional political and fiscal factors in the development of library automation, 1967-71. *Journal of Library Automation, 7*(March), 5-26.
Weinbach, R. W. (1984). Implementing change: Insights and strategies for the supervisor. *Social Work, 29*(May/June), 282-286.
Werbel, J. D. (1983). Job change: A study of an acute job stressor. *Journal of Vocational Behavior, 23*(October), 242-250.

ANNE GRODZINS LIPOW

Director for Library
Instructional Services
University of California—Berkeley

Why Training Doesn't Stick:
Who is to Blame?

ABSTRACT

This article, "Why Training Doesn't Stick," presupposes that it does
not, and that, as a matter of course, it is a waste of precious dollars to
send someone to a workshop or a seminar for training. Soon after
training goes the assumption that the trainee will be doing things the
old way. While acknowledging that at least sometimes that training
does stick, the author has come to understand that the conditions under
which training is successful are so specific and so rarely met that when it
happens it is the exception rather than the rule. "Who is to blame?" The
author answers that question by explaining how we can turn the tables
and make "training that sticks" the rule rather than the exception.

TRAINING AND CHANGE

For over two years now, this author has been trying to understand
change—what causes it, who causes it, why it is resisted, and what can be
done to help assist with moving with change and aiding to help shape it.
These are the questions that come with the territory as a developer of
in-service training programs that keep the staff up to date with the
fast-changing times. In her book, *Effective On-the-Job Training*, Sheila
Creth (1986), director of the University of Iowa Libraries, explicitly
draws the link between training and change: "First and foremost, training should be seen as a *change agent*" (p. 5).

That is, most of the programs developed or arranged for should ask
people to change their ways, to do things differently or think differently
from the way they are accustomed, in order to be effective in today's
library and in order that the library be effective in today's world. One

observation is that the majority will leave a workshop or seminar feeling good about it and wanting—perhaps eager—to apply what was learned. But, those very same people are comfortably back to their old ways a month or two later—nothing has changed.

This cannot be attributed to laziness, less intelligence, lack of desire, or fear. The phenomenon is too widespread. Though the picture is slowly beginning to change, the professional literature has not paid much attention to the problem to date, but it is a most interesting topic to examine. However, other occupations have given it some thought. They call it "transfer of training"; or sometimes "transfer failure." On the one hand, there are some interesting theoretical speculations and studies by learning theorists that shed some light. A little of that literature will be reviewed here. And on the other hand, there are practitioners, mostly personnel and management specialists, who write about how to make training stick—they don't worry about the whys of it; they just tell us what to do about it, and some of their insights will also be shared with the hope that more librarians will be encouraged to work on the problem.

CHANGE VERSUS HABITS

Change is inevitable. Throughout the history of this planet and the history of the inhabitants of this planet, there is nothing that has not changed. This is not a new revelation. How many times have you heard that "the only thing that doesn't change is change" or "the more things change the more things remain the same"; but when you think about it, that is pretty amazing.

Even an art museum docent was heard to say that art changes. I hadn't thought about it till then, but, when I did, my first thought was: "You'd think that to paint a face is to paint a face: two eyes, a nose, a mouth. How can that change? But in fact there's an Etruscan face, a Renaissance face, a Cubist face, an Impressionist face—and all are different and represent a different period in time. If change is inevitable, then why aren't we built to adapt to it? Why does there seem to be the inevitable resistance to it?

One way of seeing that we indeed are built to resist change is to think about the function that habits serve. Habits free us from having to make choices about everything in life—i.e., from having to notice or concentrate on all of life's stimuli. Habits take time to develop. It might be said that a habit is formed when learning is complete, so one can appreciate the fact that when someone is asked to do things differently, it will take time to change from the old habit. For example, it is possible to drive to and from work everyday remembering nothing about the ride because of the familiarity. Move to another place and you will find that it is some time before you do not have to think about where you are going or, going home, you will, from habit, head for your old neighborhood. Courtesy is another habit—e.g., please, thank you. Those aren't natural; we weren't born saying those words. Those aren't even commonsense things to say. We had to work at them. How often did our parents say: "Say thank you to the nice lady?"

There are, of course, bad habits—e.g., drug addiction, smoking, poor diet. From those we have some clue about how hard it is to break a habit. We know we are doing wrong, and yet it is so hard to change.

The time it takes to change is related to whether or not unlearning is required. That is, as we go through life, we are constantly learning new things and creating new habits. And that generally goes well when we haven't had to break old habits. Automatically fastening a seatbelt might be one example of this: a new driver will take to seatbelts much faster than an old driver because the new driver has not developed the habit of entering and starting a car without first going through the motions of fastening a seatbelt.

But when it comes to breaking old habits to attain the same goal in a new way or to abandon one behavior and substitute another, the problem becomes more complex. It is not a matter of just new learning. It requires disconnecting from old learning. The longer it took to gain the old learning, the longer it will take to disconnect from it—to unlearn it. An example would demonstrate that axiom vividly: you are given a task to perform that you had never done before, and you are timed as to how long it takes you to do it. You repeat the task several times, and with each repetition you perform the task in less time and thereby develop a kind of habit. Then you are asked to do the task in a new way. It will take longer to perform the task in a new way than it took to perform it the first time when there were no preconceived impressions to dispel.

CHANGE TAKES TIME

So unlearning is a contributor to resistance. Unless you are very motivated, the odds are that you will give up. Rationality doesn't necessarily enhance motivation. Some know well the benefits of seatbelts, but it takes a law to make us wear them.

Let us now examine how unlearning contributes to resistance. Learning theorists divide learning into four stages:

Stage 1: Unconscious Incompetent (UI). You are not even aware there is something to be learned (e.g., skill, theory, and its applications).
Stage 2: Conscious Incompetent (CI). You are aware there is something to be learned.
Stage 3: Conscious Competent (CC). You learn the skill, concepts, and procedures and can apply what you learned with mistakes and omissions.
Stage 4: Unconscious Competent (UC). You can perform well without thinking about it.

How to get from the CC stage to the UC stage is the trick. Most retreat before they get to the UC stage. The reason is that the route from

CC to UC is unpleasant: we must become incompetent for a time and must do so in the eyes of people who regarded us as competent; we must abandon attitudes and practices that worked rather well and were efficient in favor of attitudes and practices which are uncomfortable and which make us temporarily inefficient. We must disconnect the neurological ruts we once created so as not to have to think before we act—in other words, we must unlearn—so as to be able to begin the long process of forming new neurological ruts.

When in a slump in learning development, we are usually unaware of learning theory that would explain that the slump is natural and expected and that the big payoff is just around the corner. Perhaps we are simply on the "forgetting" side of a normal learning curve, and by sticking with it we enter the very rewarding "relearning" phase.

For example, a competent typist is sent to be trained in word processing. The first day back from training it takes her six hours to type a one-page letter that could have been completed in five minutes on a trusty electric typewriter. In this CC stage, the typist has taken a giant step backward. You can understand why it is likely she will abandon the effort, even though she may be aware that if she became a UC, she would perform at a higher level than when she was an UI.

So change—that is, learning to do something a new way—takes time and more time than we realize. It takes more time than a training session and more time than a week of training sessions. It requires time to unlearn and time to be incompetent. Once these facts are accepted, half the battle is won. Progress is made toward preventing transfer failure. Or, the other way around, we are moving toward ensuring training transfer. In addition to time, two other factors need to be in place for change or training transfer to be successful: (1) the trainee's commitment to change, and (2) the supervisor's (or institution's) commitment to change.

Trainee's Commitment to Change

The trainee needs to have a strong commitment to change. A. J. Anderson (1985/86) in an interesting article in *Journal of Library Administration* in which he examines change in managers from a psychoanalytic standpoint, describes the views of M. Scott Myers (1970) in *Every Employee a Manager*. Discussing why it is so difficult for managers to change, Myers claims that knowledge of management theories rarely leads to changed behavior. Deliberate and intensive efforts must be made to apply the theories. Using a slightly different learning stages model from the UI to UC model, Myers says:

> "the application of theory generally requires a four-step process:
> Step 1. Awareness
> Step 2. Understanding
> Step 3. Commitment to change
> Step 4. New habits
> The first step, *awareness*, may result from reading a book or article, attending a

workshop, listening to a convincing speech. The person gains superficial insight into a new theory and the implied deficiency in his or her present way of doing things. Step two, *understanding*, may result when the person recognizes a possible need to change. This is the "intellectual condition" stage. The person might read [more] and attend seminars and training programs, even to the point of becoming an articulate spokesperson on behalf of the theory, but his or her management style continues to follow old habit patterns [the 'do as I say, not as I do' type].

The next step, *commitment to change*, is a most important one in the process. It occurs when the person becomes aware of the discrepancy between his newly adopted theory and his everyday behavior, and believes he will benefit personally through changing his behavior. (Anderson, 1985/86)

Anderson (1985/86) says that: "Myers points out that initial attempts to change are often discouraging, and if not reinforced by some type of rewarding feedback, may be abandoned." Finally, step four, the *new habits* step. "New habits are established when sustained deliberate application of the new theory finally results in attitude changes and automatic and natural expressions of the desired changes in style of management." For change in management style, getting through stage 4 can take five to ten years. Most people, according to Myers, never progress beyond step 2.

What Myers and Anderson are describing is not limited to managers trying to change their style. For any significant change in behavior, going beyond step 2 requires "sustained deliberate application" of new learning. Anderson sums up the problem well: "students or workshop participants must assume responsibility for their own learning." (You can lead a horse to water but you can't make it drink.) Anderson's words are "nothing will happen to those who do not persevere." And if you read enough into "nothing," you might decide that he is giving out a death sentence.

To be taught is not necessarily to learn. As Anderson (1985/86) puts it: "The laws of habit formation hold true in the mind as they do in the body....Why is it that so many people you know seem to remain the same regardless of the number of courses they have taken? Why do they present one style to the world and never deviate from it....[Can] people remake themselves as a result of taking courses and attending workshops[?]....These questions raise the issue of what education can and cannot accomplish." Anderson (1985/86) concludes that it is not easy to change: "*some* people *can* change *certain* aspects of themselves and their behavior IF they *want* to badly enough, and if they are *willing* to *work* hard enough at it. The key words here are *some, can, certain, want, willing,* and *work.*" On the grounds that we are made up of a combination of traits—some inborn and related to physical makeup, some relating to intellect; and other traits derived from our surroundings, experiences, and other external influences—Anderson looks to physiologists Ernst Kretschmer and W. H. Sheldon, psychologists Freud and Jung, and philosopher Edouard Spranger for enlightenment.

They all categorize human beings into personality types. And in one way or another, they all conclude that modifications must lie within the boundaries of one's original type-nature. For Anderson, that is why the emphasis on certain people can change if they want to badly enough. There is no question that attitude and motivation have a great deal to do with whether one is capable of changing their behavior and practices. "That proverb 'You can take a horse to water, but you cannot make it drink' applies here....You can take a student to the classroom, but you cannot ensure that the things you wish to impart will be assimilated. For this to happen a person must want to change....[The students'] cooperation with the teacher in the learning process is essential....Given our basic natures, where thinking tends to harden into habit and where behavior takes on a relatively fixed form, progress from the old to the new can be accomplished only in the face of much mental and emotional resistance. Old mind sets have to be resolved into a hospitable flexibility in order that new attitudes and expectancies may be formed. *This takes time* [emphasis added]."

When library training programs are measured against time standards such as these, it doesn't give a person much time. Ruth Clark (1986), California Edison training manager, says that "even after an excellent class, training frequently fails to pay off in behavioral changes on the job" (p. 83). She says that people go back to work and do it the way they have always done it instead of the way they were taught in the class. This phenomenon is called "transfer failure." "It happens," says Clark (1986), "because skills do not transfer automatically into job performance. In other words, the fact that you have learned how to do something a certain way doesn't necessarily mean you'll do it that way. Since the point of job-related training is to improve performance on the job, transfer failure obviously defeats the whole purpose" (p. 83).

Supervisor's or Institution's Commitment to Change

Dana Robinson and James Robinson (1985) put the responsibility for transfer of training on more than the trainee: "Skills are transferred when both the learning experience and the work environment work together to achieve the same results. The following formula captures this concept: LE x WE = Results" (pp. 82-83). LE refers to learning experience and describes the learning activity in which the learner participated. The trainer is responsible for this part of the equation. WE represents the work environment of the learner; the day-to-day environment in which the learner works following the program. "Line management must ensure that the environment supports, reinforces and rewards the learner for using the new skills and knowledge. A zero on either side of the multiplication sign yields a zero in sustained results from training" (p. 82). Most libraries score zero on the WE side.

Becky Schreiber (1985), independent consultant in Maryland, gets more specific about this follow-up back in the work environment. She argues for ensuring on the job coaching to help a trainee who has returned from a workshop to practice the skills learned (pp. 123-24). Much like an athletic coach, she wants someone there to encourage, provide reinforcement, and offer constructive corrective advice as one goes about their work. "The likelihood of transferring skills without coaching is low." Until performance reflects new skills, it cannot be said that the skills have been learned (p. 133). "To set up a coaching experience, there needs to be teamwork among three key individuals— the seminar participant, her/his supervisor, and the seminar leader.... [Participants] must be willing to shed their professional roles and their need to be seen as fully competent so that they can become students again" (Schreiber, 1985, p. 123). (Consider again the stages of learning: becoming a student again—the CC stage—means showing yourself as less than competent. You can see why the prospect of becoming a CC would be a big part of the reason why there is resistance.

Also, "if participants are...clear on which skills they intend to learn, they will demonstrate a high level of personal initiative about learning these skills and be better focused on how they can use them on the job" (Schreiber, 1985, p. 123). Skills transfer is given its best chance, according to Schreiber (1985), when

—coaching opportunities—during and after the workshop—are built into the design of the training workshop;
—there is a clear understanding and agreement between workshop leader and participants about content and methods of the seminar;
—before leaving the workshop, participants do specific strategy planning with action steps and time lines. This is an opportunity for participants to anticipate the barriers that may prevent them from using their new skills;
—back-on-the-job coaching begins as soon as they return from the workshop and continues till learning is completed and new behavior is formed. A key consideration here should be the comfort of the staff member. There needs to be a high level of trust between the trainee and coach so that risk-taking occurs and genuine constructive feedback is provided and self-confidence develops. The immediate supervisor may serve as coach if the relationship reflects that kind of trust. Sometimes, however, the dual responsibility of coaching and evaluating is difficult for the supervisor. Supervisors should be encouraged to examine this dilemma with a bias toward seeing both roles as a staff development function of their jobs. If they are unable to resolve the issue, it would be difficult for the supervisor to be a good coach;
—feedback is recognized as a primary tool of the coaching experience— feedback about both successes and failures (pp. 123-24).

Michael Kruger and Gregory May (1985), in their article "Two Techniques to Ensure that Training Programs Remain Effective," express the problem of training transfer in terms of investment and return. They look at the amount of money organizations spend in training—e.g., $40.6 million is spent each year in the federal government alone just in training managers—and conclude that "these invest-ments indicate that organizational decision makers place a high priority on this type of training. Yet that investment often represents an expres-sion of faith since the link between what is learned in the classroom and what is applied on the job is usually tenuous" (p. 70). Two conditions must be met, they claim, to increase the likelihood that the training investment actually results in a return at the workplace: *relevance to needs* and *reinforcement mechanisms* (p. 70). Relevance—that is, train-ing that meets the needs of participants—"boosts motivation to learn. Thus the level of readiness to learn, the so-called 'teachable moment' is heightened" (Kruger & May, 1985, p. 70). But training programs must also be reinforced: "They must also include strategies that enhance the application of learning in the workplace" (p. 70). Though organiza-tions regard training as critical, as demonstrated by the amount of time and money invested in it, paradoxically, Kruger and May (1985) main-tain that, "it is the exception rather than the rule for organizations to expend the effort needed to ensure that a reinforcement of learning will occur at the workplace following the training" (p. 70).

Change, Or Else...

You might ask why this is so important now. It seems that more noticeably than ever, the library, just like everything else, is changing—big changes and fast-happening changes—and it's happening with or without us. All the thinkers of the profession tell us that. Pat Battin (1984) has said that: "Far from being extinct in the electronic university, librarians will be in greater demand than in the more serene and organized world of the book" (pp. 12-17). Richard De Gennaro (1984) said that: "The emphasis in libraries is shifting from collections to access. Providing access to information will be the principal goal and activity, and coping with technology and change will be the principal driving forces of the emerging information age library" (p. 1205). Kevin Hegarty (1985) (director, Tacoma Public) has said that: "The entire organizational structure of a library will be affected by the automated system, and the method of doing business will be drastically changed" (p. 43). Marilyn Mason (1985) (from the public library sector) stated that: "Within ten years over half of the service provided to library users will be to individuals who never come into the library" (p. 137).

Richard Rowe (1987), president and CEO of Faxon, in an "On My Mind" column in *American Libraries* was more provocative in his predictions about change. He bluntly states that librarians today aren't ready to manage in this fast-changing world of information. Frankly, he says, librarians "do not have much of an edge in qualifying for that CIO [chief information officer]...."

> We can't just sit back and see the future happen and think that we are going to have an important role in the future simply because of the importance of information, or because of the past importance of libraries. That won't be enough...librarians must change. We're going to have to be open to new ideas.

We are going to have to stretch ourselves and take some risks....[We can't assume that] since we've been in the business for 20 years we know what our users want....We've got to let go of current assumptions about our roles. We've got to keep our eye on the long term value of why we are here. (Rowe, 1987, p. 297)

Rowe (1987) ends with: "Change is inevitable. Change is an opportunity for things to go better or worse. It's up to us to make those decisions and to do it now."

Of course, even if all these important people never said a word, we know the statements are accurate; we can see it before our eyes. Who has the same job they had five years ago? If your present job existed five years ago, did the previous person do things in the same way as they are done now? Probably not. If you've been in the current job for a while, are newly-hired coworkers required to have skills or approaches different from yours? If asked to guess what differences there would be in your job five years from now, you might not be able to come up with a crystal ball answer, but it would probably be difficult to say "I doubt there'll be any changes." What do you think those changes will be and how do you plan to prepare for them?

What about people who don't want to change? There is much concern about that. At an ALA/LAMA/PAS program on "Training Issues in Changing Technology," Ruth Person, associate dean at Catholic University of America, talked about "human factors in adopting library technology." She said, "change itself is problematic for many individuals....[While there are] several categories of individuals who *embrace* change in the adoption of innovation (innovators, pacesetters), [there are] far more individuals who approach the change process with everything from hesitancy to real fear....Individuals may fear being displaced, disconnected from old patterns, dehumanized by machinery" (Person, 1986).

A leading head reference librarian in a large academic library and known for her forward thinking, competence, and innovation, confided that she will retire next year at age 55, much earlier than she would have thought. She hates what is happening in reference—i.e., sitting at a keyboard and having a database regurgitate is boring to her. The excitement of discovery, moving from place to place and back again, is what brought her into the profession, and she sees that as becoming passe, not just for librarians but for researchers. She worries that new researchers will become passive and understand research to be whatever is findable at their fingertips and deliverable to their door through a document delivery service. She thinks the online medium encourages new and terrible habits based on implied assumptions they lead you to come to.

PRACTICAL STEPS TOWARD ACHIEVING TRAINING TRANSFER

Now that it is understood why training does not stick and what the solutions to the problem are, what would an effective training program look like in a library setting? The following are ten conditions that an effective library training program should meet in order to ensure training transfer:

1. The training program should be relevant to the needs of the trainee and should be perceived as relevant by the trainee.
2. There should be a three-way agreement about the objectives of the training program among the trainee, the trainer, and the trainee's boss.
3. There should be a three-way agreement about the expectations of the trainee among the trainee, the trainer, and the trainee's boss.
4. Supervisors or higher-level managers ideally should attend a session of any training program they are planning for those who report to them.
5. Supervisors and trainees should plan the program follow-up.
6. A supervisor or a higher level manager should agree that there will be no blame for a trainee's slip-ups during follow-up practice.
7. The trainee should leave the training session with a plan specifying how specific learned skills, attitudes, theories, etc. will be practiced and applied.
8. After the workshop, the trainee should practice with a coach and preferably another workshop trainee so that they can agree to coach each other.
   Notes: Ideally, practice should begin in a nonfamiliar environment; the new surroundings should bolster the formation of new behavior and thought patterns before it becomes necessary to break old patterns.

   Coaching requires no-blame feedback and should include both criticism and praise. If the trainee is the sole person from a unit to be trained, the trainee should be expected to give a report about the training program to the home unit telling coworkers what behaviors to expect, look for, listen for, ask about when missing, etc.

   No activity worth training for should be exempt from coaching (though for some activities it will be more difficult to implement than others). Managerial training, the reference interview, telephone skills, dealing with problem patrons, and competence in computer systems are all areas for follow-up coaching.
9. The trainee should be scheduled to give a progress report two weeks, two months, and six months after the workshop—describing specific applications of what was learned.
10. The institution should strive for achieving a critical mass of staff or managers competent in the desired skill. The critical mass will have been reached when those who possess the skill set the dominant standard. (Those who do not possess the skill are then self-motivated to change and can be expected to take responsibility to close the apparent gap between them and those who possess the skill.) The sooner that critical mass is reached, the earlier the desired change will be effective and the library's desired goals will be reached.

This discussion has not covered all of the issues related to change and resistance to it, but perhaps a dimension has been added that rounds out the picture and adds to the usual explanations of resistance—i.e., fear of the unknown, a need to cling to the past, a lack of motivation—a more positive and possibly more prevalent reason—the lack of a continuing learning environment.

If change is inevitable, and if library change is happening now with or without us, it seems that anyone who can help us move with change and shape it for the better is a friend. We need all the friends we can get so that we don't become irrelevant, so that we don't leave change to "new blood" or "the youth" or to someone else, so that *we* can remain a part of the future.

REFERENCES

Anderson, A. J. (1985/86). Do people change their management styles and practices as a result of taking courses and attending workshops? *Journal of Library Administration, 6*(4), 1-14.

Battin, P. (1984). The electronic library—a vision for the future. *EDUCOM Bulletin,* (Summer), 12-17.

Clark, R. C. (1986). Nine ways to make training pay off on the job. *Training, 23*(November), 83-87.

Creth, S. (1986). *Effective on-the-job training: Developing library human resources.* Chicago and London: ALA.

De Gennaro, R. (1984). Shifting gears: Information technology and the academic library. *Library Journal, 109*(June 15), 1204-1209.

Hegarty, K. (1985). Myths of library automation. *Library Journal, 110*(October 1), 43-49.

Kruger, M. J. (1985). Two techniques to ensure that training programs remain effective. *Personnel Journal, 64*(October), 70-75.

Mason, M. G. (1985). The future of the public library. *Library Journal, 110*(September 1), 43-49.

Myers, H. S. (1970). *Every employee a manager: More meaningful work through job enrichment.* New York: McGraw Hill. (As quoted by A. J. Anderson, *op cit.*).

Person, R. (1984). Human factors in adopting library technology. Talk delivered at ALA/LAMA/PAS program on "Training issues in changing technology." (June 26), (Unpublished).

Robinson, D. G., & Robinson, J. C. (1985). Breaking barriers to skill transfer. *Training and Development Journal, 39*(January), 82-83.

Rowe, R. (1987). You, the CIO. *American Libraries, 18*(April), 297.

Schreiber, B. (1985). You can take it with you: Coaching for on-the-job application of learning. *Public Libraries, 24*(Fall), 123-124.

CHARLES MARTELL

Dean and University Librarian
California State University
Sacramento, California

Achieving High Performance
in Library Work

ABSTRACT

In this article, the concept of productivity is recast. This is necessary
because the nature of work is undergoing a profound transformation.
As a result, corporate and political leaders are seeking to build an
institutional framework in which excellence and high performance are
adopted as basic cultural norms. To be successful in this effort, leaders
must create a new reality for the employee. This must include a high
quality of work life.

Discussion of a set of critical human resource issues may help to
provide a platform from which to refocus personnel administration as it
is currently practiced in our nation's libraries. These issues are: motivation; job design; quality of work life; organizational culture; high
performance; and excellence and renewal.

INTRODUCTION

In a particularly vivid scene from one of his classic C-rated movies,
Victor Mature sits idly, chained to an oar. A new sound is heard, the slow
beat of a drum. Each of the slaves picks up the beat with his oar and the
warship moves forward. Suddenly an alarm is given. "Enemy ahead!"
The drum beats faster and the slaves row faster. Some fall to the deck
only to be whipped back into place. The individual beats of the drum
blend together and the movements of the slaves become feverish, almost
chaotic.

The slaves have but one task, to row to the beat of the drum. The
design of their jobs is elemental. They have no control. There is no place

73

for creativity or initiative. Their decision-making alternatives are two-fold: row or be whipped.

In a purposefully exaggerated sense, these slaves are simply tools for production. Their value can be measured by the single criterion of speed. Unfortunately, the message of productivity—i.e., as doing something faster—is not limited to old movies. Much of management thought since the Industrial Revolution has focused on the employee working faster.

Within our profession we often find "productivity" rated first—or second after quality—on performance review forms. The primary question is, Does the individual produce an acceptable amount of work?

One of the ironies of contemporary life in the United States is that the need for faster work is critical. Yet for America's workers the meaning of the word "productivity" has often been debased by a historical, single-minded pursuit that ignored and even rejected the needs of the worker for a reasonable quality of work life. Rights were generally reserved for management. The rights of workers were twofold: stay or leave. This certainly was a big advantage over the choices available to Victor Mature and his fellow slaves.

In this article the concept of productivity is cast into a broader framework. This is necessary because the nature of work and its corresponding performance requisites are undergoing profound changes. As a result, corporate and political leaders are examining means to create a society that strives for excellence and high performance as basic cultural norms. To be successful in achieving these goals, leaders must likewise create a new reality for the employee. This must include a high quality of work life.

A discussion of these critical human resource issues may help to provide a platform from which to refocus personnel administration as it is currently practiced in our nation's libraries. These issues are: motivation; job design; quality of work life (QWL); organizational culture; high performance; and excellence and renewal.

MOTIVATION

In a recent survey of the terms most often entered by the users of InfoTrac, "employee motivation" placed thirty-fifth. No other personnel-related term appeared among the top fifty (Higgins, et al., 1987, p. 5). An analysis of the most requested *Harvard Business Review* reprints reveals that ten out of the top twelve are on the subject of motivation. These examples provide evidence of the considerable interest in motivation (Herzberg, 1987, pp. 109-17).

Unfortunately, the concept of motivation, like that of productivity, is frequently misused. Many managers believe that motivation is an external force to be applied to the employee. This view is often expressed in terms such as, I motivate my staff to work hard. Most researchers, however, view motivation as an internal force that "energizes, directs, or sustains behavior" (Steers et al., 1975, p. 6).

Because the motivational state of the employee is probably the most critical element in achieving excellence, an understanding of some of the major theories of motivation should prove helpful to the reader (Hinrichs, 1976). These theories of motivation (see Figure 1) fall into three categories or a combination of these categories: (1) the individual, (2) the job, and (3) the work environment.

Characteristics of the Individual

Abraham Maslow (1954) found that before an individual strives for higher level psychological needs such as self-esteem or self-actualization (what a man can be, he must be), he/she must meet basic lower level physiological, safety, and belongingness needs. This means that the energizing forces of motivation would usually unfold in stages.

Those with a high need for self-actualization—often the best performers—are motivated by an internal drive to use their capacities to the fullest. Maslow refers to "capacities clamoring to be used which cease their clamor only when they are used sufficiently" (Garfield, 1986, p. 60).

Category 1	Characteristics of the Individual	*Maslow*
	What employee brings to work situation	Need Hierarchy Theory
		McClelland Achievement Motivation Theory
Category 2	Characteristics of the Job	*Herzberg*
	What employee does at work	Motivation— Hygiene Theory
Category 3	Characteristics of the Work Environment	Working Conditions, Salary, & Interpersonal Relations
	What happens to the employee at work	
Category 4	Interaction between Individual and the Work Environment	*Adams* Equity Theory
		Steers & Porter Expectancy/ Valence Theory

Figure 1. Theories of motivation

David McClelland (1976) studied the achievement orientation of individuals. Those with a strong need for achievement have high standards of excellence and are very goal-directed. They take responsibility for finding solutions to problems. They set moderate achievement goals and take calculated risks. They also want concrete feedback as to how well they are doing.

Characteristics of the Job

Frederick Herzberg (1966) did not focus on the individual. Instead, he found that the individual acquires a sense of self-actualization, achievement, and meaning from the job itself and not from the context of work, the work environment, or from what an individual brings to the job.

Herzberg described two sets of key factors: hygiene factors (job context) and motivating factors (job content). The hygiene factors include company policy, supervision, interpersonal relationships, working conditions, salary, status, and security. An employee would not experience long-term satisfaction from favorable hygiene factors, but unfavorable hygiene factors would lead to long-term dissatisfaction.

Motivating factors include achievement, responsibility, recognition, advancement, and growth. Herzberg believed that an employee would be more highly motivated over the long-term if his/her job had positive motivating factors. This approach led Herzberg to emphasize the design of jobs, an area in which he has been extremely influential. This aspect of his work will be discussed later.

Herzberg's (1968) article, "One More Time: How Do You Motivate Employees?" is the number one *Harvard Business Review* reprint. More than 1,200,000 copies have been requested.

Characteristics of the Work Environment

During the 1800s and early 1900s there was little interest in the subject of work motivation. Work conditions were often deplorable, but there were few constraints on the employer. A Fall River mill worker provides this graphic description of her work situation:

> At first the noise is fierce, and you have to breathe the cotton all the time, but you get used to it. Lots of us is deaf—weavers—that's one reason I couldn't get that second girl place. The lady said I couldn't hear the door bell if it would ring, but you never think of the noise after the first, in the mill. Only it's bad one way: when the bobbins flies out and a girl gets hurt, you can't hear her shout....She's got to wait till you see her. (Barnum, 1971, p. 27)

As the social conscience shifted and as a new managerial class emerged, concern about the negative effects of poor working conditions on employees and their levels of motivation became a significant social issue. This interest lessened in the 1930s and 1940s as experts looked more closely at group dynamics and the psychology of the worker (Sundstrom, 1986, p. 62). Lately, however, there has been renewed interest in what happens to the employee at work. Figure 2 depicts a variety of conditions that affect work—e.g., lighting, climate, and the ergonomics of the workplace. These conditions may influence the amount of worker satisfaction and work outcomes.

As an example, many library employees have begun to complain about the eye strain, headaches, and back strain that they are experiencing because of their work on computer terminals. This has become a significant problem. On the one hand, the problem can be cured easily with the appropriate equipment and scheduling. On the other hand, some managers turn a deaf ear to such concerns.

Likewise, the potential stressful situations that might arise from electronic supervision are not always acknowledged. The Computer and Business Equipment Manufacturers Association (CBEMA) in its *Industry News* points to the benefits of this type of monitoring. The CBEMA does not acknowledge, nor has it seen any research proving, that computer monitoring may produce undue stress (Computer & Business Equipment Manufacturers Assn., 1987).

Interaction of the Individual and the Work Environment. In his article, "Inequity in Social Exchange," J. Stacy Adams (1965) states that "inequity exists for Person whenever he perceives that the ratio of his outcomes to inputs and the ratio of Other's outcomes to Other's inputs

Noise	Work Content	
Lighting	Autonomy	
Temperature	Chance for Advancement	
Color	Peer Relations	
Air Quality	Physical Environment	Job Satisfaction
Equipment	Job Security	
Privacy	Salary	
Status Symbols	Company Policies	
	Supervision	

Adapted from Eric Sundstrom. (1986). *Work places: The psychology of the physical environment in offices and factories.* New York: Cambridge University Press (p. 80).

Figure 2. Work environment and job satisfaction

are unequal." The existence of an inequity creates a tension which the individual handles by: (1) altering his inputs and outcomes, (2) distorting his inputs and outcomes cognitively, (3) leaving the field, (4) acting on other, and (5) changing the object of his comparisons.

Positive inputs may relate to variables such as age, sex, ethnicity, and education. Positive outcomes include rewards intrinsic to the job, satisfying supervision, and benefits. Negative outcomes include poor working conditions, monotony, and several of Herzberg's dissatisfiers.

Expectancy/valence theory focuses on the relationships among inputs—the interaction between the individual and the work environment—rather than on the inputs themselves. The major inputs, or the determinants of performance in the organizational setting, are motivational levels, abilities and traits, and role clarity (Steers & Porter, 1975, pp. 180-86). "This theory argues that motivational force to perform—or effort—is a multiplicative function of the expectancies, or beliefs, that individuals have concerning future outcomes *times* the value they place on those outcomes (Steers & Porter, 1975, p. 181).

Summary

The subject of employee motivation is extremely complex. Furthermore, despite all the research that has been conducted and the thousands of articles that have been written, the various theories fail to complement one another. Rather, they seem to confound one another. This makes it very difficult to synthesize findings from the literature and from practice so as to have something of solid, pragmatic value.

Because of the importance of this issue, however, guidelines or hints for action need to be offered. Some hints may be easier to make than others. Recently, while in the staff room, an employee was overheard repeating aloud the title of an article she was reading, "How Do You Raise Your Self-esteem?" Quick as a flash, I replied: "Climb a ladder!" There was a certain amount of satisfaction with this retort, but this humorous advice had little value to others. This is often true of the statements of many of those in the "motivation" advice business.

Self-esteem is serious business. The California Task Force to Promote Self-Esteem and Personal and Social Responsibility has a budget of $245,000 a year for three years, courtesy of taxpayers. Its charge is to explore the relationship between low self-esteem and major social ills. One member, Jack Canfield, says: "My work in education is all about self-esteem" (Matthews, 1988, A-1, p. 22).

As was noted earlier, the people who usually provide motivational advice—this group may occasionally include academic researchers—are always inventing something new. Meanwhile, in real life situations, we are searching frantically for practical solutions. The best advice is to treat your employees with respect and provide them with meaningful work; include an opportunity for them to discover and use an inner drive to make a contribution and to find recognition for their efforts.

Design of Work

Herzberg writes that the simplest and easiest way to get something done is to ask somebody. He finds that employers typically did not deal with employees in this way. Instead, they use a kick in the pants. Herzberg also believes that people should not associate movement with motivation. Motivation comes from within; it is not imposed externally. Management's role is to set the conditions by which the internal motivation of the employee may be energized and sustained (Herzberg, 1987, pp. 109-20). Edwin Locke (1970) writes:

> A supervisor can help fulfill an employee's desires but he cannot provide him with desires; he can offer him new knowledge or the chance to gain new knowledge but he cannot force him to learn; he can assign goals to a worker but he cannot compel him to accept those goals.

In libraries we may want employees to make a greater personal investment, but we must also work together to establish a balanced organizational investment. This investment should include work that is designed to: (1) bring out the best qualities in our employees, (2) have a high quality of work life, and (3) encourage the pursuit of excellence within a high performance organizational culture.

Historically we have not taken this approach. People have often been treated as tools or as extensions of machines. This led managers to ignore the unique characteristics of the individual employee. Frederick Taylor saw that this practice was dysfunctional in several ways. For example, it overlooked the physiological differences between employees. He was able to demonstrate successfully that a tall worker with a short-handled shovel was not likely to be as productive as a tall worker with a long-handled shovel. With this insight Taylor began to design tools that were the right size and weight for typical categories of employees. The customizing of tools for the worker had a dramatic impact and fostered the emergence of the science of ergonomics.

Despite the genuine improvement in working conditions, the psychological makeup of employees remained generally irrelevant until the 1930s. The attitude that employees are mere instruments still has many adherents although there is increasing recognition of the intrinsic value of human resources.

The effective design of jobs can elicit higher levels of employee motivation. This usually has a positive effect on satisfaction and performance. In this section, several forms of job design will be discussed briefly. Readers are referred to other material that the author has written on this subject. J. Richard Hackman's (1975) job enrichment model will also be described.

Flex-time, work simplification, job rotation, and job sharing are four of the most common types of job change. These changes affect either the context of the job, or, in the case of work simplification, make the job easier and less challenging. Their motivating potential is weak at best (Martell, 1981; Martell, 1983, pp. 43-65).

Another common job change strategy is to add tasks or to increase the variety of tasks. This is called job enlargement. Herzberg (1987) called it the enlargement of meaninglessness.

To make a job meaningful it is necessary to add five core job dimensions: skill variety, task identity, task significance, autonomy, and feedback (Hackman, 1975, pp 57-71). If this is done, the employee is able to experience three critical psychological states: meaningfulness of the work, responsibility for outcomes of work, and knowledge of the actual results of the work activity. By designing work in this direction, the self-esteem and self-actualization of employees often increase dramatically.

Core job dimensions and critical psychological states are factors in Hackman's (1975, pp. 57-71) job enrichment model. In this sense, job enrichment is the process by which a person gains greater control over the factors that directly affect his/her job (Martell & Untawale, 1983).

—*Scheduling*: when you do what during the day;
—*Decision-making*: meaningful involvement in the decisions that affect your tasks, your job, and your role within the library;
—*Meaning*: who does your work help and how important does it seem to you; and
—*Feedback*: the information that you receive on how your efforts contribute to the goals of your unit, the library, and, most importantly, users.

What must you change? Hackman (1975) suggests that you: combine tasks; form natural work units; establish client relationships; add autonomy; and open feedback channels (pp. 42-44). By making these changes you will increase the levels of motivation and satisfaction, achieve higher work quality, and lower absenteeism and turnover (Yorks, 1976).

The rationale behind some of these suggested changes may need an explanation. For example, why is *establish client relationships* included? Quite simply, an organizational structure that is formed around clients would tend to place as many librarians as possible in a direct relationship with the clients. Combined with autonomy and the implicit control and decision-making authority that results, the source of the librarian's satisfaction or dissatisfaction is focused not on management but on the client or library user (Herzberg, 1987, p. 120).

To achieve, sustain, and expand one's excellence, it is necessary to know how you are doing on a continuous basis. This explains why *feedback* is such a critical job design factor. In librarianship the library is usually structured around function and rarely, if ever, around client. Also feedback is normally provided during retention, promotion, and tenure cycles. Rarely do librarians receive direct and objective—i.e., unbiased—feedback on the quality, effectiveness, and performance characteristics of their (1) lectures or other types of library instruction presentations, (2) online search skills, (3) collection development expertise, (4) reference skills, and (5) committee work.

Within the profession there are few librarians who know anything about job design techniques and even fewer who have practiced these techniques. This is a serious problem if the profession is to make excellence and high performance one of its norms in not only a symbolic sense but also in a strict pragmatic sense. To do so will be difficult. First, there are the design techniques that must be learned and implemented. Second, there are the norms in our professional culture that must be modified. A few issues related to the former will be discussed here. Organizational culture will be discussed in a later section.

A job is made up of multiple tasks. To redesign the job of even one employee can be complicated. The situation becomes more complex when one realizes that the concept of job is limited in comparison to the concept of organizational role. Librarians, for example, have roles that frequently include librarywide and campus assignments, creative and scholarly activity, community service, professional service, and personal development.

A library has several levels. It may be necessary to redesign more than one job in a unit in order to bring overall relationships and roles into a reasonable symmetry. To move beyond one unit will require the cooperation of additional supervisors and employees. Larger organizational issues may also come into play as the scale of a redesign effort is expanded.

Change efforts are complicated by the fact that organizations have multiple levels: task, job, unit, department, division, and the library as a whole. For example, to redesign one job in one unit takes both a lot of work and a very knowledgeable librarian. Such a librarian might be able to redesign the work of all employees in his/her department. However, the very success of this effort might lead other department heads to feel challenged or even threatened. Frequently, over time, the innovative department is forced to retrench and the innovation fails. It has been demonstrated that in order to provide a supportive climate for work redesign, organizational values throughout the library must be favorable and congruent.

The problem of expanding from the design or redesign of one job to multiple jobs or units led to the development of more sophisticated concepts and techniques for improving the effectiveness of work through job design. One of the most popular terms is work systems design. The term is broad enough to encompass a total organizational-wide job/role change effort. At this point, it is time to call in a consultant and ask for advice. The complexity is beyond the scope of this article. Large-scale changes have been reported in the literature and may interest some readers (Ford, 1979; Glaser, 1976; Katzell et al., 1977; Walton, 1979).

Quality of Work Life

If libraries are to make important strides forward, library employees must be willing to make significant personal investments in this effort. Their willingness to do so is strengthened if libraries accept corresponding obligations. Guarantees of a high quality of work life represent one such form of investment.

QWL Definition

One popular definition of quality of work life is: "the degree to which members of the work organization are able to satisfy important personal needs through their experience in the organization (Suttle, 1977, p. 4). These personal needs can be satisfied through the design of jobs that include six major QWL characteristics: autonomy; challenge; expression of creativity; opportunity for learning; participation in decision-making; and use of a variety of valued skills and abilities.

QWL Predictors

From the answers to a survey asking: "What aspects of working life do organizational members consider important?" Mark Levine et al. (1986) compiled seven predictors of QWL:

—challenge in my work;
—degree to which my superiors treat me with respect and have confidence in my abilities;
—extent to which my life outside of work affects my life at work;
—extent to which the work I do contributes to society;
—self esteem;
—variety in my daily work routine; and
—work at present leads to good future work opportunities.

Library employees, who respond positively to these predictors, are likely to have a high QWL and are most likely to support new policy, service, and performance initiatives (Martell, 1985; Martell & Creth, 1984; Martell & Kunselman, 1984; Martell & Holbrook, 1984; Martell & Swanson, 1984; Martell & Tyson, 1985; Martell & Gorman, 1983; Martell, 1983a; Martell & Johnson, 1983).

Any discussion of QWL in libraries must make a clear distinction between librarians and other staff. The professional model that covers librarians parallels the QWL model and its attributes; however, staff are not the beneficiaries. A two-part (professional-staff) strategy is therefore necessary for achieving high performance in library work.

Some very thorny questions arise here. For example, is QWL appropriate for some employees but not for others—e.g., for librarians but not for other staff? If some QWL approaches advocate lowered status differentials among employees—e.g., participation by all staff in decision-making—will some librarians reject QWL? Or the definition of QWL is stated in terms of what the employee needs. What about the organization's needs? (In the following sections there will be some clarification of what the organization needs.)

A case could be made that, in general, many librarians already have a high QWL, especially if compared to workers in other sectors of the

U.S. economy. If so, have they responded by demonstrating significantly higher performance norms, or a closer orientation to the client in the sense implied by Thomas Peters and Robert Waterman (1982), the authors of *In Search of Excellence*, and others? Would researchers or social commentators identify librarians or libraries as having the strong competitive dynamic typical of excellent organizations?

In the 1960s, a number of articles described the underutilization of librarians. It was difficult to understand how this situation might exist in a "healthy" profession, one that, at least in theory, espoused high levels of autonomy and personal control. Today, it is apparent that librarians are not underutilized, but they may be poorly utilized. Whatever the exact condition of the profession in terms of degree of utilization, many would agree that dramatic, perhaps profound, changes are underway. In "EIDOS and the Transformation of Libraries," Frederick Kilgour (1987) states:

> By the end of the century, however, librarians, even though they surely will not have discarded bibliography and its associated printed materials, will be well out "beyond bibliiography," [*sic*] and the focus of their professional concern will be to treat each user as an individual even to the extent of supplying them with information before they seek it. (pp. 46-49)

Being close to the client is one of eight prescriptive characteristics of excellent organizations according to Peters and Waterman (1982). To become excellent it is necessary to be responsive. This means the continuous monitoring of the external environment: (1) to learn about changes in the client's needs, and (2) to develop new programs and services in response to these changes (Hearn & Heydinger, 1985). However, the organizational structure of libraries and professional norms limit severely the degree to which libraries can and have been responsive to clients' (users') needs (Martell, 1983b).

Therefore, even if QWL becomes an institutional norm, there is little reason to believe that professional norms, or other relevant norms, would change as a direct result. What is still needed is the creation of a library culture that has among its basic norms: high performance; responsive, client-driven services and programs; a strong tendency toward innovation; and an urge to excel.

ORGANIZATIONAL CULTURE

The culture of an organization consists of the learned behaviors and shared meanings of its members and their transmission to new members. After the first day of practice with his new team, the Seattle Seahawks' Brian Bosworth, former All-American linebacker from the University of Oklahoma, spoke to reporters about professional football's acculturation process. "It's more finesse out here for some reason. At Oklahoma, we were programmed all the time to bite the hell out of people" (Associated Press, 1987a, p. C-13).

In libraries there is rarely any talk of a "bite the hell out of people" philosophy. The profession's competitive energies lean toward finesse. To achieve excellence, however, librarianship may need a competitive drive that is more analogous to business and sports than to its traditional heritage.

As an example, librarians rarely use the word "productivity" except in its most pejorative sense. To talk about the number of books cataloged per hour by a cataloger is to move outside of accepted professional norms. The concept is not accepted culturally. There have been discussions about standards, but these relate to what should be done and how, not to how many. Also, in the area of reference, librarians avoid through various forms and strategies any effort to determine the quality of reference service.

Curiously, reference librarians measure quantity (how many questions they receive per hour), but not quality (how effectively these questions are answered), while catalogers measure quality (how well the books cataloged conform to relevant standards), but not quantity (how many books they catalog per hour).

In "Finding the Culture of Productivity," Gib Akin and David Hopelain (1986) show that the most productive employees do what no one else thinks is possible, things you wouldn't expect. These employees have internal levels of initiative and excellence that are not taught to them by others in the same situation. Other elements in a productive environment include: effective teamwork; identification with the job; results oriented; support for accomplishment; using skills autonomously; and willingness to work hard.

An examination of the culture of libraries is necessary to determine if it matches society's requirements and those of users. To improve this culture, librarians may have to go to the user's place of work and determine what the user needs and how the library can be responsive to these needs.

Each of us is going to have some variation in perspective about the pressing issues facing libraries and the practical responses that need to be undertaken. Building a more productive culture is but one of the cultural changes that appear necessary. Other changes in culture would lead the profession to encourage and facilitate creativity, risk-taking, experimentation, and entrepreneurship.

Many supervisors, including library supervisors, have a strong need to know exactly what is going on at all times. To accomplish this they may establish restrictive, often subtle, controls about what is considered appropriate staff behavior (Feldman, 1985; Martell, 1987). This orientation may lead them to react negatively to employee initiatives.

Recently, after a presentation on motivation and excellence, a library manager in the audience asked about how to handle a perplexing situation that she had faced. "In my department we were discussing some basic technical processing routines when a staff member made some observations that we thought were creative. I really wonder whether or not we should take these kinds of risks." This author was taken aback. The level of risks that we normally face in libraries is minor. To think that a library employee is at risk with her colleagues because she offers a creative approach is foreboding.

Still, many of us face related perplexing situations. For example, in some libraries resources are so tight that each decision takes on added meaning. There is too little opportunity to experiment. This particular year, in the library budget at California State University, Sacramento (CSUS), there was no money budgeted for projects. Indeed, as a manager it may seem necessary to be overly careful in a fiscal sense at the very time that experimentation and risk-taking are required in order to take advantage of new opportunities.

If libraries are to be key players in the so-called knowledge industry, administrators, librarians, and staff must discover within themselves new sources of creativity and motivation. Finding these new sources runs parallel to efforts at the national level. Indeed, one reason for the deep interest in the issues of creativity and motivation, as well as excellence and productivity, is the serious deterioration in the competitive position of the United States. A lowered standard of living might result. This nation's libraries and the profession of librarianship would suffer enormously.

HIGH PERFORMANCE

What do we want our employees to do? If the answer is to produce more, then productivity is the key issue. If we want high quality, then quality control may be the most important issue. If the decision is made to emphasize excellence, then a more sophisticated framework would be most helpful.

First, there are basic (productivity) factors—how many, how fast, how good. Second, there are intermediate (performance) factors—how efficient, how effective. Finally, there are advanced (excellence) factors. The advanced factors relate to the basic mission of the library. They place the library within an encompassing social context. This context includes: the social utility of the library as an institution; the degree to which the library enhances our democratic processes and the skills and aptitudes of our population; the benefits of the library to the process of scholarly communication; and the contribution of the library to the creation and application of knowledge.

At an EDUCOM workshop during the national conference in Los Angeles (October 1987), a speaker who is on the faculty at a prestigious library school defined libraries as if they were solely collections of things. In his view, the role of librarians is to provide bibliographic access to library collections. This viewpoint is not unique. It places an instrumental value on human resources—i.e., as the extension of a tool—the collection.

This historical perspective is also grounded in the culture of the library profession itself. There is sufficient evidence to support the belief that most librarians would put their personal value in second place after the collections in their libraries. This attitude distorts the "true" value of libraries to society. We have also adopted a set of cultural norms that limits our ability to see objectively another reality (or realities) that holds greater promise for the future of libraries.

A relatively crude analogy may help to put this abstract concept into focus. Assume that how the profession treats the collection is analogous to how Detroit treats the automobile: "make the item (book or automobile) available to a user/customer." What is missing in the Detroit approach? It ignores:

—impact of cost of purchase on customer—e.g., monthly payments, car insurance, reduction in savings rate;
—maintenance costs to be absorbed by user;
—purpose of use—e.g., family car, dune buggy, cheap used car for student;
—safety of the car—e.g., child locks, emergency braking distance;
—pollution controls;
—gasoline consumption;
—comfort and other ergonomics;
—appropriateness of tires for environmental conditions; and
—satisfaction factors.

In addition to the multiple impacts that the purchase and use of the automobile have on the user, it is obvious that there are significant social issues—i.e., the energy dependency of the United States, air quality, health care, quality of life, employment rates in the industry, state of the Gross National Product, and trade balances.

Library collections serve purposes that are equally as varied and frequently as meaningful. Service practices and their conceptual underpinnings, however, have a low value-added ratio in comparison to potential approaches.

High performance is an important need in many organizations. Performance in one sense relates not so much to efficiency or how fast somebody did something, but to effectiveness or the degree to which the work performed allows the organization to achieve its goals. However, as Rosemary DuMont (1980) suggests, librarians have had difficulty defining organizational effectiveness because they have not been able to define library goals in a satisfactory manner.

High performance means working harder, but it also means to work smarter and better. Many librarians work hard already. Many don't have much more to give. Library managers need to discover new paths, and because they are unlikely to get new resources, managers must find innovative ways to shift human resources within a consensual framework. Arie P. DeGeus (1988) calls for institutional learning—"the process whereby management teams change their shared mental models of their company, their markets, and their competitors."

Presently, many employees worry when management starts talking about something new. A discussion with management today may lead to a perceived wild-eyed scheme to add a new workload on top of an already burdened staff with the commitment of already overcommitted resources. Also, who will do the work? Not management!

In trying to build a collaborative but high performance work environment, managers must adopt more advanced attitudes about their primary resource, people (Alcott, 1987, p. E-1). Recent studies have shown that workers are generally happy with their jobs, but they are not happy with management. Of employees in one study, 53 percent were satisfied with salaries. Other favorable ratings were: benefits (61 percent satisfied), physical environment (61 percent satisfied), job satisfaction (70 percent satisfied). However, as regards management treatment, only 39 percent were satisfied. Obviously many employees hold critical attitudes toward their supervisors/managers (Associated Press, 1987b, p. D-2; Goleman, 1987, p. D-1-21).

An understanding of what factors create satisfaction or stress for the employee can assist efforts to progress toward higher levels of performance. Charles Bunge (1987) reports that patrons were the main source of stress among the librarians that he studied. Patrons were also the main source of satisfaction. Support staff reported that their main source of stress was supervision. Relations with other colleagues were another major source of stress for the support staff. Support staff may have higher needs for affiliation to offset the lack of recognition and autonomy that are associated with their positions.

Because monetary rewards are limited, it becomes more necessary to create challenging work so that the intrinsic needs of the employee are recognized and met more clearly. Each employee should establish a set of high performance goals. Once this is completed, the appropriateness of the goals should be reviewed. Keith Bell (1983) suggests that we ask ourselves the following questions:

—Are my goals realistic?
—What are the odds of my reaching my goals?
—Are my goals measurable?
—Is the payoff worth the price?
—Have I outlined a likely road to success?
—How much control do I have over reaching my goals?
—What are the opportunities that exist?
—Are there other ways of reaching my goals? (pp. 78-79)

Measuring attainment or progress toward goals is an important characteristic of sports. Sports figures know when they have done something well: they win or lose. Librarians and other staff need to develop similar benchmarks if high performance is to become a cultural norm.

In many roles, personal achievement is the result of excellent teamwork. Managerial success is predicated on the teamwork of others. For this reason managers must have a clear sense of their role (Tichy & Devanna, 1986). A clear role definition is the first prerequisite for the development of a well-constructed set of personal goals. Richard Steers and Lyman Porter (1975) state that each manager should:

—Take an active role in managing motivation processes at work—through conscious, intentional behavior.
—Be aware of your own strengths and weaknesses and your role in the organization.
—Increase your sensitivity to variations in employees' needs, abilities and traits.
—Be able to identify superior performers and reward them.
—Improve job and role clarity of your staff.
—Increase the amount of attention paid to the quality of the work environment, including group dynamics and organizational climate.
—Assess the attitudes of your staff on a continual basis as a motivational barometer.
—Allow employees to participate more fully in processes aimed at attaining organizational effectiveness. (pp. 558-59)

In summary, the roles of librarians and libraries are narrow when one views the profession from a knowledge society perspective. Achieving high performance in the context of this article implies both a major shift in the nature of library work and in the performance characteristics of the profession (Zuboff, 1985; Strassmann, 1985; Hirschhorn, 1984; Beniger, 1986). The need for structural changes in the profession mirrors a national outcry about the structure and activity of our economy. For example, Lester Thurow and others have recently written books on the reindustrialization of America (Thurow, 1985; Bowles, et al., 1983; Wachter & Wachter, 1984). They are developing new concepts about how the nation's economic resources should be deployed and managed.

EXCELLENCE AND RENEWAL

The profession of librarianship is at a crossroad. It has the potential to adopt a far different, more proactive service orientation than we have in the past. Also, the new technologies offer some very interesting possibilities—e.g., compact discs and data files. This is a historic juncture. However, the various technologies often intersect with one another and create a confusing pattern.

In "Corporate Leadership Skills: A New Synthesis," Richard Byrd (1987) lists several formerly popular terms for describing leadership styles—e.g., Theory X and Theory Y, Theory Z, Beyond Theory Z, the Blake and Mouton managerial grid, and Likert's System 4 manager. Every few years there is a new theory to grab onto.

Byrd (1987) avoids the tendency to create his own theory but he does describe several skills that are necessary for those who wish to exert a leadership role:

—*Anticipatory Skills*—An effective leader intuitively and systematically scans the environment for potential areas of exposure to new historical risks.
—*Visioning Skills*—The skills associated with visioning entail creating mental and verbal pictures of desirable future states, persisting and persevering, and sharing and creating a new reality with others.
—*Value-Congruence Skills*—Corporate leaders must be in touch with their employees' psychological, economic, safety, spiritual, sexual, aesthetic, and

physical needs. In this way, they can engage employees on the basis of shared
motives, values, and goals.

—*Empowerment Skills*—The skills associated with empowerment entail
being willing to share power; taking delight in others' development more
than in having control; and realizing that visions are achieved by teams, not
by single leaders.

—*Self-Understanding Skills*—[These] skills entail being willing to search for
personal identity and growth, appreciating that personal ego strength is a
requirement for leading, being open to feedback and other performance
data, and having a frame of reference by which to understand and arouse
motivation.

With the realization of these skills it will be possible to say, as does
Tom Peters (1988) in "Traditional Management Notions Take a Brutal
Beating," "the for-so-long comfortable world of management practice
has truly been turned upside down" (p. E-2). Tom Peters was also one of
the authors of *In Search of Excellence*. The other was Robert Waterman
(1987a) who recently completed a new book *The Renewal Factor*. In it
he recommends that change be adopted as the basis for all of our activity.

Waterman is especially interested in what makes an organization
excellent. He found that goal-directedness is a key factor in high performance. Renewing companies:

> Turn tedious issues into a noble cause....They do so in ways that enhance the
> dignity of the people they employ.
> Porsche CEO Peter Schultz brings the point to life with this story: "Three
> people were at work on a construction site. All were doing the same job, but
> when each was asked what his job was, the answers varied. 'Breaking rocks,'
> the first replied. 'Earning my living,' said the second. 'Helping to build a
> cathedral,' said the third."
> Few of us can build cathedrals. But to the extent we can see the cathedral in
> whatever cause we are following, the job seems more worthwhile. (Waterman,
> 1987b, p. 120)

In libraries we often think of our roles as checking out books and
answering reference questions. Yet we have a cathedral of knowledge in
our institutions. We need to orient services to unlock that knowledge for
patrons. This gives us a real challenge, a challenge that requires the
highest levels of performance, excellence, and renewal (Gardner, 1984).

REFERENCES

Adams, J. S. (1965). Equity in social exchange. In Leon Berkowitz (Ed.), *Advances in experimental social psychology*. New York: Academic Press.

Akin, G., & Hopelain, D. (1986). Finding the culture of productivity. *Organizational
Dynamics, 14*(Winter), 19-32.

Alcott, M. J. (1987). Best bosses? They're abundant. *Sacramento Bee*, (October 4), E-1.

Associated Press, Seattle's Boz learns new concept: Finesse. (1987a). *Sacramento Bee*,
(August 16), C-13.

Associated Press, Workers happy with jobs, but not with bosses. (1987b). *Sacramento Bee*,
(August 30).

Barnum, G. (1971). The story of a fall river mill girl. In L. Stein & P. Taft (Eds.), *Workers
speak: Self portrait*. New York: Arno and the New York Times.

Bell, K. F. (1983). *Championship thinking: The athletic guide to winning performance in
all sports*. Englewood Cliffs, NJ: Prentice Hall, Inc.

Beniger, J. R. (1986). *The control revolution: Technological and economic origins of the
information society*. Cambridge, MA: Harvard University Press.

Bowles, S., et al. (1983). *Beyond the wasteland: A democratic alternative to economic decline.* Garden City, NY: Anchor Press.

Bunge, C. (1987). Stress in the library. *Library Journal, 112*(September 15), 47-51.

Byrd, R. E. (1987). Corporate leadership skills: A new synthesis. *Organizational Dynamics, 16*(Summer) 34-43.

Computer and Business Equipment Manufacturers Association. (1987). *Industry News,* (September 22), 1-2.

De Geus, A. P. (1988). Planning as learning. *Harvard Business Review, 2*(March/April), 70-74.

DuMont, R. R. (1980). A conceptual basis for library effectiveness. *College & Research Libraries,* 41(March), 103-111.

Feldman, S. P. (1985). Culture and conformity: An essay on individual adaptation in centralized bureaucracy. *Human Relations, 38*(April), 341-356.

Ford, R. N. (1979). *Why jobs die & what to do about it: Job redesign & future productivity.* New York: AMACOM.

Gardner, J. W. (1984). *Excellence: Can we be equal and excellent too?* (rev. ed.). New York: N. W. Norton.

Garfield, C. (1986). *Peak performers.* New York: Avon Books.

Glaser, E. M. (1976). *Productivity gains through worklife improvements.* New York: Harcourt Brace Jovanovich.

Goleman, D. (1987). The curse of rotten bosses. *Sacramento Bee,* (January 4), D1-2.

Hackman, J. R. et al. (1975). A new strategy for job enrichment. *California Management Review, 17*(Summer), 57-71.

Hearn, J. C., & Heydinger, R. B. (1985). Scanning the University's external environment. *Journal of Higher Education, 56*(July/August), 419-445.

Herzberg, F. (1987). One more time: How do you motivate employees? Reprint and comments in *Harvard Business Review, 65*(September/October), 109-120.

Herzberg, F. (1968). One more time: How do you motivate employees? *Harvard Business Review, 46*(January/February), 53-62.

Herzberg, F. (1966). *Work and the nature of man.* New York: Hartcourt.

Higgins, C. et al. (1987). InfoTrac usage research report (Exhibit 5). (June 26). Belmont, CA: Information Access Co.

Hinrichs, J. R. (1974). *The motivation crisis: Winding down and turning off.* New York: AMACOM.

Hirschhorn, L. (1984). *Beyond mechanization: Work and technology in a postindustrial age.* Cambridge, MA: MIT Press.

Katzell, R. A. et al. (1977). *A guide to worker productivity experiments in the United States 1971-75.* Prepared for work in America Institute Inc. New York: New York University Press.

Kilgour, F. G. (1987). EIDOS and the transformation of libraries. *Library Journal, 112*(October 1), 46-49.

Levine, M. F.; Taylor, J.; & Davis, L. E. (1984). Defining quality of work life. *Human Relations, 37*(January), 81-104.

Locke, E. A. (1970). The supervisor as "motivator": His influence on employee performance and satisfaction. In B. M. Bass et al. (Eds.), *Managing for accomplishment.* Lexington, MA: Lexington Books.

Martell, C. R., Jr. (1987). The nature of authority and employee participation in the management of academic libraries. *College and Research Libraries, 41*(March), 110-122.

Martell, C. R., Jr. (1985). QWL strategies: People are the castle, people are the walls, people are the moat. *Journal of Academic Librarianship, 10*(6), 350-354.

Martell, C. R., Jr. (1983a). QWL strategies: Trust, subtlety, & intimacy. *Journal of Academic Librarianship, 9*(3).

Martell, C. R., Jr. (1983b). *The client-centered academic library: An organizational model.* Westport, CT: Greenwood Press.

Martell, C. R., Jr. (1981). Improving the effectiveness of libraries through improvements in the quality of working life. *College & Research Libraries, 42*(September), 435-446.

Martell, C. R., Jr., & Creth, S. (1984). QWL strategies: Toughness. *Journal of Academic Librarianship, 10*(5).

Martell, C. R., Jr., & Gorman, M. (1983). QWL strategies: Reorganization. *Journal of Academic Librarianship, 9*(4), 223-225.

Martell, C. R., Jr., & Holbrook, C. (1984). QWL strategies: Managing participation. *Journal of Academic Librarianship, 10*(1), 29-32.

Martell, C. R., Jr., & Johnson, H. F. (1983). QWL strategies: Investing in people. *Journal of Academic Librarianship, 9*(1), 33-35.

Martell, C. R., Jr., & Kunselman, J. (1984). QWL strategies: Involvement = commitment. *Journal of Academic Librarianship, 10*(3), 158-160.

Martell, C. R., Jr., & Swanson, P. (1984). QWL strategies: Consideration. *Journal of Academic Librarianship, 9*(6), 350-351, 382.

Martell, C. R., Jr., & Tyson, J. (1985). QWL strategies: Quality circles. *Journal of Academic Librarianship, 9*(5).

Martell, C. R., Jr., & Untawale, M. (1983). Work enrichment for academic libraries. *Journal of Academic Librarianship, 8*(January), 339-343.

Maslow, A. H. (1954). *Motivation and personality.* New York: Harper & Row.

Matthews, J. (1988). Self-esteem task force feels good about itself. *Sacramento Bee,* (February 21), A-1, F-22.

McClelland, D. C. (1976). *The achievement motive* (includes a new preface with hindsight (1950-1975) by John W. Atkinson). New York: Irvington Publishers.

Michael, L. W., & Susan, M. W. (Eds.). (1984). *Removing obstacles to economic growth.* Philadelphia: University of Pennsylvania Press.

Peters, T. (1988). Traditional management notions take a brutal beating. *Sacramento Bee,* (February 17), E-2.

Peters, T. J., & Waterman, P. H., Jr. (1982). *In search of excellence: Lessons from America's best-run companies.* New York: Harper & Row.

Steers, R. M., & Porter, L. W. (1975). *Motivation and work behavior.* New York: McGraw Hill.

Strassmann, P. A. (1985). *Information payoff: The transformation of work in the electronic age.* New York: Free Press.

Sunstrom, E. (1986). *Work places: The psychology of the physical environment in offices and factories.* New York: Cambridge University Press.

Suttle, J. L. (1977). Improving life at work—problems & prospects. In J. R. Hackman & J. L. Suttle (Eds.). *Improving life at work: Behavioral approaches to organizational change.* Santa Monica, CA: Goodyear.

Thurow, Lester C. (1985). *The zero-sum solution: Building a world-class American economy.* New York: Simon and Schuster.

Tichy, N., & Devanna, M. A. (1986). *The transformational leader.* New York: John Wiley & Sons.

Walton, R. E. (1979). Work innovations in the United States. *Harvard Business Review, 57*(July/August), 88-99.

Watcher, M. L., & Watcher, S. M. (1984). *Removing obstacles to economic growth.* Philadelphia: University of Pennsylvania Press.

Waterman, R. H., Jr. (1987a). *The renewal factor: How the best get and keep the competitive edge.* New York: Bantam Books.

Waterman, R. H., Jr. (1987b). The renewal factor: Causes and commitment. *Business Week,* (September 14), 120.

Yorks, L. (1976). *A radical approach to job enrichment.* New York: AMACOM.

Zuboff, S. (1985). Automate/informate: The two faces of intelligent technology. *Organizational Dynamics, 14*(Autumn), 5-18.

CHARLES A. BUNGE

Professor
School of Library and Information Studies
University of Wisconsin—Madison

Stress in the Library Workplace

ABSTRACT

This article provides information on organizational approaches to managing stress in the library workplace; defines stress as a person's psychological and physiological response to the perception of a demand or challenge; develops the concepts of stressors and coping strategies; and emphasizes the importance of library personnel officers, administrators, and managers knowing the dynamics of stress in the lives of individual workers and having awareness of the important sources of stress in the library workplace. The discussion also treats strategies for reducing stressors, assisting staff members in developing good stress management, and helping the employee who is at risk of burnout.

INTRODUCTION

Stress in the workplace is currently a topic of great interest. For example, there is increasing awareness that excessive stress can be hazardous to employees' health, and stress, as a cause for disability, can obligate employers and their insurers to worker compensation. Ineffective management of stress can lower the productivity of individual employees and, as a result, of an entire organization.

This article will discuss some aspects of stress in the library workplace. It will not attempt a thorough review of the literature, either of stress in the workplace in general or of stress in the library workplace. Rather it will provide overview information, along with library examples that the author has come to believe is important to library managers and personnel officers. The article includes both concepts and information that are widely accepted from the literature of stress management and insights drawn from discussions with a great many working librarians and library managers. After providing some basic definitions and concepts regarding the phenomenon of stress, the article will then discuss sources of stress in the library workplace. Finally, organizational strategies for dealing with such stress will be discussed.

BASIC CONCEPTS

The term or concept of *stress* is defined in widely varying ways in the popular press and among researchers and clinicians who have studied the phenomenon (Bailey, 1985; Cherniss, 1980; Farber, 1983; Freudenberger et al., 1980; Maslach, 1982). Some treat it as an intrinsically painful or negative phenomenon and one to be avoided, while others consider it to be potentially either positive or negative depending on the situation. The definition on which this article is based considers stress to be a person's psychological and physiological response to the perception of a demand or challenge. The nature and intensity of this response depends on the meaning one gives to the demand or challenge and on one's assessment of the resources that are available for meeting it.

This conception of stress has a number of important elements. First, stress is not something "out there" or inherent in "stressful" things or situations. Rather, stress is within the person—i.e., a response. The source of the demand or challenge is referred to as a "stressor." A stressor with negative meaning (the source of undesirable stress) for one person may cause a completely different response in another.

Another element in this definition of stress is the importance of the person's *perception* or way of thinking about the situation. Surely, few normal persons would wish to be without demands or challenges; these can be part of the joy and verve of life. However, some demands will be perceived as potentially harmful or uncomfortable, and the response to these demands will be an attempt at avoidance or reduction. Likewise, one will sometimes feel that one has adequate skills and other resources to deal with a demand, and the response may be one of pleasurable anticipation. On the other hand, a feeling of not having adequate resources to meet a demand can be an occasion of worry or other painful response. Such a painful or negative response is often called "strain" or "distress."

From this definition it follows that managing the amount and nature of stress in one's life consists of attempting to achieve a balance between the challenges and demands of one's life and the resources available to meet these challenges. When we feel that there are too many demands or too few resources to deal with them, we will experience excessive or painful stress (i.e., strain or distress).

Another important concept associated with stress is *coping*. In the context of this discussion coping can be defined as an individual's attempt to reduce or master the pain or discomfort associated with stress.

Broadly speaking, coping strategies include getting away from or reducing the number of stressors, obtaining more resources to meet demands, and changing one's perceptions of the situation. For most people, most of the time, the coping strategies used are effective, and stress is kept at a level that allows happy, productive functioning. However, sometimes the coping strategies used are not effective. In fact, they can contribute to the problem in a vicious circle way. For example, some responses to a perception of having too much work to do and too little time and resources in which to do it actually reduce productivity and thereby increase the frustration and pain for the worker.

To the extent that a person's coping strategies are generally ineffective and the "vicious circle" strategies are out of control, the person can be said to be "burned out." Stress, distress or strain, and burnout can be viewed as a continuum. This continuum runs from: (1) a condition wherein, on the whole, challenges are sources of happiness and productive responses, to (2) a condition wherein perceived imbalances between demands and resources are painful, but where coping strategies restore the balance and reduce the pain, to (3) a condition where inappropriate coping strategies are out of control (i.e., are contributing to the problem) and the person's physical and mental resources are depleted.

SOURCES OF STRESS IN THE LIBRARY WORKPLACE

From this conception of stress and burnout, one can see that stress may be either functional or dysfunctional in the workplace. Logic would predict, and there is some research to show (e.g., McGrath, 1976), that performance and productivity will improve with increasing stress to a certain level, after which increased stress will cause lowered performance. The interactions among individuals, organizations, and jobs that produce stress and distress in the workplace are very complex. Each employee is unique with regard to the meanings one attaches to stressors, perceptions of available resources, and the coping strategies and skills one can and will use. Each organization is, likewise, unique with regard to the stressors it contains or produces and its approaches to helping employees manage and cope with stress.

There is a large body of literature on sources of stress in the workplace which includes public service organizations (Beech et al., 1982; Brief et al., 1981). Reports to this author from some 850 library staff members from all types of libraries and library positions confirm that the library workplace has much in common with jobs in other organizations (Bunge, 1987). The following discussion will cite sources of stress in the library workplace.

Certainly one of the chief causes of stress is work overload of a quantitative or qualitative nature. In many libraries budget cutbacks and staff shortages have caused staff members to feel that there is always more work to do than there is time to do it (quantitative overload). For example, public services staff members express this in terms of too many requests for service to allow thorough or adequately tailored responses to any of them. Technical services staff members feel the pressure of never seeing the "in" basket or the shelf of materials to be processed diminish or of always having to accomplish special projects without reductions in "regular" work expectations.

In addition to the sheer quantity of work, library staff members may feel a qualitative overload. For example, they often feel that their job requires knowledge and skills that they do not have, that the job contains elements that are inappropriate, or that the job is frustratingly fragmented or complex. Reference librarians report feelings of inadequacy regarding their knowledge of information sources and technology, impatience with "nonreference" duties such as dealing with "problem" patrons and maintaining photocopy machines, and conflicts between on-desk and off-desk duties. Technical services and support staff feel qualitative overload in terms of lack of knowledge and skill (in computer use, for example) to do their jobs, or of always having to balance a variety of disparate tasks, some of which they may feel are inappropriate to their positions.

What might be called work underload can also be a source of stress for library staff members. Some library jobs, especially for support staff, can be repetitive, unchallenging, and lacking in meaningful stimulation. Reference librarians frequently report being disappointed that so many reference questions they receive are routine or even trivial. Technical services librarians often feel that their jobs allow too few opportunities for them to use their creativity and the skills they have acquired through training.

Another broad category of stressors in the library workplace is interpersonal relationships. Relationships with library patrons are an obvious source of stress for public services staff members. On the one hand, there can be great intensity in relationships between librarians and the people they try to help, sometimes leading to feelings of inadequacy and frustration when the help cannot be fully responsive to the patron's needs. On the other hand, patrons can sometimes be rude or ill-behaved, can seem to expect miracles, can steal or mutilate materials, or can otherwise cause stress for the public services librarian.

Library staff members are also distressed at a lack of respect and recognition in their interpersonal relationships. Public services librarians and administrators usually report this as a lack of recognition of the library's role and value by people outside the library. Technical services librarians and support staff more frequently report feelings of lack of appreciation and respect from others within the library.

Beyond the lack of recognition and respect, interpersonal relationships among library staff members in general are an important source of stress. Examples reported to the author include interdepartmental conflicts, tensions between professionals and nonprofessionals, competition for status and resources, irritable and negative co-workers, and gossip.

Consistently high on the list of reported stressors in libraries is the lack of effective positive feedback from supervisors, co-workers and patrons. Evaluation from supervisors is often seen as infrequent, not timely, based on inadequate data, and ineffectively communicated. Co-workers (especially from other departments or levels of staff) are perceived as more likely to make complaints than to give compliments. Patrons often seem to take public services librarians for granted and fail to let them know when the information provided is helpful.

Related to evaluative feedback and recognition is the matter of expectations from others felt by library staff members. Often library workers feel that the expectations for their jobs are vague and poorly defined. Perhaps even worse, there seems sometimes to be conflicting expectations. For example, reference librarians often feel that the library administration and the taxpayers expect them to be all things to all people, while the allocation of time and other resources (and perhaps even performance evaluation criteria) demand setting priorities and limiting services—often in the absence of clear policy guidelines. Examples of such role ambiguity and role conflict are not limited to reference librarians, and they can be very stressful to all types and levels of library staff members.

Another set of perceptions that usually appears on a list of stressors for library staff members is that of inadequacies in supervision and management. Inadequacy in evaluative feedback has already been mentioned; other examples include supervisors who are absent or inaccessible when information or support is needed, feeling left out of decisions where one has important knowledge or expertise, managers who will not risk advocating strongly for their staffs, inconsistent or double standard supervisory behavior, and managers who allow (or force) their staffs to gain important information from the grapevine.

Of course one would expect that working conditions would be a major source of stress in the workplace, and that is true for the library workplace. Inadequate office space is a frequently mentioned stressor of this type, especially crowding and lack of privacy in shared offices (e.g., what is called the "reference office" in many libraries might better be called the "reference bullpen"). Libraries usually reserve the most attractive spaces (e.g., those with windows) for patron-use areas, leaving less attractive space for staff. Library work areas are prone to having a cluttered appearance and can be noisy, both of which can be stressful.

A final category of sources of stress in libraries to be mentioned might be called career stage or career concerns. Entry, midcareer, and approaching retirement are career stages that have particular stressors and potential burnout associated with them. For example, in the public services professions, including librarianship, the early months and years in one's career can be filled with the stress caused by the gap between the realities of the job and the expectations that were built up during training.

Middle managers are particularly prone to painful stress and burn-out. They are especially likely to feel role ambiguity and role conflict. Often the demands of their positions have risen faster than have their competence and skills. They frequently report feeling caught between demands (from both above and below) and the lack of resources to respond to them.

A very important example of this category of stressors in libraries is the vulnerability of working women to distress and burnout. The useful article by Brief, Schuler, and Van Sell (1981) on working women and stress might have been written about library staff members, according to reports to the author from women workshop participants (pp. 173-201). Reported stressors range from discrimination against women in hiring, pay, and promotion to sex-typing of certain jobs within libraries, to child care and housekeeping issues and pressures.

Organizational Responses to Stress

How can libraries as organizations, including their policymakers, managers, and personnel officers, deal with stress and burnout in the workplace? Organizational strategies can be grouped into several categories including: (1) reducing the number and intensity of stressors, (2) strengthening the employees' ability to cope with stress effectively, and (3) recognizing and assisting those who are not coping effectively and who are at risk of burnout. The goal of such strategies is not the complete elimination of stress or strain but rather the maintenance of stress at a level with which individuals can cope effectively and productively.

Reducing Stressors

The earlier discussion of sources of stress in the library workplace suggests many areas for reducing stressors. Remedies for reducing stress in organizations have been discussed by several professionals such as Cherniss (1980); Jackson et al. (1983); and Sethi and Schuler (1986). Stressors associated with quantitative and qualitative work overload can be reduced through job redesign—the topic of another article in this issue. Managers, working with staff, should try to arrange the employee's day so that intense or taxing activities alternate with other activities for variety and relief. Duties that are inappropriate to the employee's role or training (e.g., equipment servicing by reference librarians) should be kept at a minimum. The number of hours worked at intense or exhausting tasks should be carefully limited, and jobs should be structured so as to allow workers to take "time outs" when necessary. Opportunities for learning, for using creativity, and for innovation should be built into jobs to the greatest extent possible. Staff members should be encouraged to take vacations, and the accrual of unused vacation time should not be treated as an object of pride or status. Stress resulting from competition can be reduced by developing work strategies that are collaborative rather than competitive—for example cross-departmental team efforts.

Many of the stressors that are related to interpersonal relationships, role ambiguity, and role conflict, can be addressed through good organizational communication. Library administrators should assess the degree to which all staff members receive clear, timely, and full information relevant to their jobs and their contributions to the organizational mission. Identified gaps and deficiencies should be remedied. Policies, goals, rules, and expectations should be made as clear and explicit as possible for each staff member. Timely evaluative feedback, especially of a positive and supportive nature, should be provided to each employee.

Feelings of helplessness and lack of control or power are serious stressors in the workplace. Library managers should provide staff members with the maximum feasible autonomy and control over their work including participation in collective decision-making.

Clearly managers and supervisors play a very important role in reducing and controlling stress in the library workplace. Libraries need to create management and supervisory training and development programs that include stress management knowledge and skills. Among areas to be addressed would be problem-solving and conflict resolution skills, effective evaluation techniques and skill in communicating evaluative feedback, group leadership skills, motivation toward risk taking and advocacy, decision-making and follow-through abilities, and knowledge of how stress affects individuals and of effective coping strategies.

Library managers, personnel officers, and others in authority should continually monitor the physical work environments of staff members for sources of stress and strain. Many librarians have reported to the author that a great deal can be done to enhance the feeling of privacy and comfort rather inexpensively through furniture rearrangement, the use of movable screens, and the personalization of workspaces. Attention to reduction of clutter and noise (from both people and machines) can reduce stress significantly. Attractive paint and decoration can partially compensate for lack of windows. Proper lighting and physical arrangements of equipment and work stations are very important, especially where computer terminals are involved. The area of physical surroundings is an especially good example of one where staff members can be provided with a sense of control and power over their work lives. Helping workers themselves approach these stressors in a problem-solving way and helping them turn their decisions into actions and changes will not only reduce the stressors but will make the staff members feel better about themselves and their work and more able to cope with irreducible stress.

Many of the stressors in the library workplace come from what was referred to earlier as career concerns or career stages. This category of stressors can be reduced by improving the fit between characteristics and competencies of individuals and the demands of the jobs they hold, as well as the fit between the expectations of individuals and the possibilities and realities of their positions. This begins with effective screening in the hiring process, for example, separating appropriate dedication and commitment from unrealistic idealism and overcommitment.

Orientation programs for new entrants into librarianship are especially important. Personnel officers need to be aware that the new professional's initial experiences play an important role in later development, and libraries should develop and implement orientation programs that will make the "reality shock" of initial experiences as constructive as possible. Such orientation programs should help staff members match their expectations to their positions and reduce anxiety about lacking skills and knowledge.

Midcareer employers, middle managers (especially women managers, and those approaching retirement) also need special assistance in reducing stress and strain. Personnel officers and top administrators should be knowledgeable about developmental stages in careers and the special stressors that are associated with the various stages. Here, again, one strategy is seeking fit between individuals and the jobs they are expected to perform. Libraries should explore the development of dual career tracks and associated reward systems so that those who lack administrative interests and aptitudes can have satisfying and high status careers in the technical or service areas of librarianship.

It is very important that library managers are as well trained as possible for carrying out their complex responsibilities, so that job demands do not rise faster than competence, thereby contributing to strain. Training in dealing with pressure, conflicts, crises, and change should be included. Managers (especially women managers) who must deal with perceptions of discrimination, isolation, and conflicts between professional and personal concerns, should be encouraged and assisted in developing support networks through peer counseling, mentoring, and other means.

Helping Workers Manage Stress

While every library staff member should feel that sources of stress are kept at a minimum in the library, even in libraries where this is successful, there will still be considerable stress in the workplace. Effective individual stress management and coping strategies are as important, if not more so, as organizational reduction of stressors. Libraries as organizations can play an important role here, too. In overall terms, this is a matter of helping employees gain knowledge, self-awareness, and skills. Works that contain useful information on helping workers manage stress include Paine (1982), Pines (1981), and Tanner (1983).

The first step to effective stress management is gaining knowledge of how stress operates in one's life and the role that various types of stressors and coping strategies can play in painful stress or strain. Libraries should help their staff members gain such knowledge through workshops and other means.

Using this knowledge, staff members can assess the sources and level of stress or strain in their own lives. Personnel officers and managers can be helpful in this regard by making available stress and burnout "checkup" or assessment instruments that have proven useful. Especially important is assistance to employees in assessing how realistic are the goals they have imposed on themselves and encouraging them to adopt more realistic goals and expectations of themselves.

The development of an effective social support system is especially important for individual stress management and coping. Such a support network can provide self-esteem, feedback and appraisal of the situation, information and advice, and assistance in making changes in the situation. Managers should be alert for opportunities to encourage and assist in the development of such support systems for staff members. Enhancing consultative approaches, group problem-solving, and team efforts can be helpful in this regard. With appropriate leadership and role modeling, staff meetings can contribute to social support and networking by providing opportunities for staff members to express themselves, to discuss stress and barriers to effectiveness, and to develop problem-solving skills.

Staff members who become aware of sources of stress in their work and lives will identify skills that they need to cope with this stress happily and productively. The library's staff development program should include opportunities for developing such skills. One such important set of skills has already been mentioned—i.e., self-awareness and reflection skills. Another very important set is interpersonal communication skills, including skill at expressing one's feelings honestly and directly, listening and empathy skills, skills at providing positive feedback, and assertiveness skills. Other skill areas that are frequently identified as important in coping with job stress are time management, relaxation, and problem-solving.

Helping Those Who are Burning Out

Even with the best programs for reducing stress in the library workplace and assisting staff members in developing stress management skills, there will be staff members who seem not to be coping well and to be burning out. Glicken (1983) and Niehouse and Mihovich (1984) focus on helping workers who are burning out. What can or should personnel officers and managers do in such situations? The first step, of course, is recognizing that there is a problem. Managers and personnel officers should be knowledgeable concerning signs and symptoms of excessive stress and ineffective coping. These include rigidity and resistance to change, boredom and apathy, procrastination and indecisiveness, constant fatigue and exhaustion, irritability and a "short fuse," chronic minor physical ailments, and overall lowered productivity. Supervisors should be alert for changes in the behaviors and attitudes of staff members. Significant changes in the frequency or intensity of behaviors such as those just mentioned and a seeming inability to "bounce back" can signal poor coping with strain.

Having identified a situation where intervention and assistance seems appropriate, the manager or other caring staff member will need to exercise confrontation skills in a supportive way. The focus should be on work expectations, inadequate productivity, and behaviors of concern rather than on personal problems, ascribed motivations, and side issues. The tendency of persons suffering from excessive stress to deny that there is anything wrong and to be somewhat paranoid or supersensitive makes this confrontation process all the more difficult and demanding of sensitivity and skill.

The knowledgeable manager or personnel specialist can assist the burning out employee in assessing the situation, including identifying sources of stress, the individual's coping strengths and weaknesses, and alternatives for developing an action-oriented plan for revitalization. While some organizations have successfully instituted counseling programs to assist employees in coping with stress (and larger libraries might want to consider this approach), individual managers should not enter into a psychotherapy or personal counseling stance, since a working or supervisory relationship is not compatible with a therapeutic relationship. Nor should the manager or confronter *prescribe* burnout workshops or therapy. Such action would further undermine the individual's feeling of autonomy and control, and participation in such activities will be more effective if it is voluntary and self-motivated. Rather, the stance of the manager should be one of providing concern, heightened awareness, information, and alternatives.

There are some specific actions that the manager might suggest or undertake. One might be to make changes in the potential burnout victim's job and responsibilities in order to reduce stress and increase prospects for the individual's revitalization. Extending deadlines and suggesting a vacation might be useful strategies. Many more possibilities are implied in the earlier section on reducing stressors in the workplace. Any such actions, however, must be undertaken in a way that will not be viewed as punitive, and the staff member should be allowed a choice in the particular strategies chosen and their implementation.

This article has attempted to provide useful information on organizational approaches to managing stress in the library workplace. It emphasized the importance of library personnel officers, administrators, and managers knowing the dynamics of stress in the lives of workers, awareness of the important sources of stress in the library workplace, strategies for reducing such stressors, assisting staff members in developing good stress management, and sensitively helping the employee who is at risk of burnout. In all of this, it is important that everyone in the organization recognize that stress can be the fire that provides energy for the joy of accomplishment and productivity. However, if the employee lacks sufficient resources to manage and control this fire he/she can eventually suffer from burnout. But even then, as Herbert J. Freudenberger (1980) says in one of the best books on stress, in every fire, even a burned out one, there are glowing embers (p. xxii). Our job sometimes, as caring people, is to help those we care for rekindle the spark and to stay afire without burning out.

REFERENCES

Bailey, R. D. (1985). *Coping with stress in caring.* Oxford, England: Blackwell Scientific Publications.

Beech, H. R.; Burns, L. E.; & Sheffield, B. F. (1982). *A behavioural approach to the management of stress: A practical guide to techniques.* New York: John Wiley & Sons.

Brief, A. P.; Schuler, R. S.; Van Sell, M. (1981). *Managing job stress.* Boston, MA: Little Brown.

Bunge, C. A. (1987). Stress in the library. *Library Journal, 112*(September 15), 47-51.

Cherniss, C. (1980). *Staff burnout: Job stress in the human services* (Sage studies in community mental health, #2). Beverly Hills, CA: Sage.

Cherniss, C. (1980). *Professional burnout in human services organizations.* New York: Praeger.

Farber, B. A. (Ed.). (1983). *Stress burnout in the human service professions.* New York: Pergamon.

Freudenberger, H. J., & Richelson, G. (1980). *Burn-out: The high cost of high achievement.* New York: Anchor, Doubleday.

Glicken, M. (1983). A counseling approach to employee burnout. *Personnel Journal, 62*(March), 222-228.

Jackson, S. E., & Schuler, R. S. (1983). Preventing employee burnout. *Personnel, 60*(March-April), 58-68.

Maslach, C. (1982). *Burnout: The cost of caring.* Englewood, NJ: Prentice Hall.

McGrath, J. E. (1976). Stress and behavior in organizations. In M. D. Dunnette (Ed.), Handbook of industrial and organizational psychology (pp. 1351-1395). Chicago: Rand McNally.

Niehouse, O. L., & Mihovich, M. (1984). Setting up an in-house program for the rehabilitation of burnout victims. *Management Review, 73*(February), 27-28, 41-43.

Paine, W. S. (Ed.). (1982). *Job stress and burnout: Research, theory and intervention perspectives.* Beverly Hills, CA: Sage.

Pines, A. M.; Aronson, E.; & Kafry, D. (1981). *Burnout: From tedium to personal growth.* New York: Free Press.

Sethi, A. S., & Schuler, R. (1984). *Handbook of organizational stress coping strategies.* Cambridge, MA: Ballinger.

Tanner, L. A. (1983). Middle management stress: Recognizing and treating burnout victims. *Healthcare Financial Management, 37*(January), 12-22.

FREDERICK DUDA

Head Librarian
New York City Tribune
New York, New York

Developing Compensation Systems in Academic Libraries

Abstract

Compensation, stated succinctly, is what employees get in exchange for their work. The adequacy of the compensation has great impact on the ability of an organization to meet its goals. Inadequate compensation leads to poor performance, absenteeism, excessive turnover, grievances, and strikes. Although such problems will never completely disappear, morale can be positively affected if an organization has formulated and disseminated its compensation objectives.

The purpose of this article is to provide background on a complex personnel specialty rarely covered in library schools. The fundamentals for designing and administering a compensation program are covered. Emphasis is given to job evaluation systems, merit-based reward systems, compensation administration, and current issues and problems in compensation management, including governmental and societal influences.

Introduction

The technological revolution of the past twenty years has caused profound changes in the function of academic librarians and enabled some to obtain the status and recognition formerly held only by their faculty colleagues. In some instances, academic librarians have exceeded faculty in salary compensation. All of this has come about during a period of great social change and fiscal constraints.

The academic librarian of the mid-1960s was underpaid, still bound by the routines and traditions of the late nineteenth century, and subservient to the power and influence of faculty and administrators.

103

We have come a long way, but we rightly continue to despair over academic librarians' role in society, the ability to recruit the best and brightest of college graduates, and the alleged meagre financial rewards.

We continue to debate the nature of the profession and sometimes question our professional status. Writing just before the outbreak of World War I, Justice Brandeis (1914) defined a profession as:

> an occupation for which the necessary preliminary training is intellectual in character, involving knowledge and to some extent learnings, as distinguished from mere skill; which is largely pursued for others, and not merely for one's self; and in which the financial return is not the accepted measure of success. (p. 2)

Whether or not one accepts Justice Brandeis's definition, we assume that librarianship is a profession and that, like professionals in other fields, we pursue it largely for others, whether these others be society as a whole or the clientele of the parent institutions. We assume further that a measure of success must entail appropriate remuneration. Academic librarians are not—if they ever were—passive reactors to faculty or institutional pressures and demands. However, librarianship is a service profession and ranked low like teaching, nursing, and social work. As unlikely as it is that academic librarians will ever attain the salaries and the prestige of lawyers, doctors, or corporate executives, they have in many cases surpassed the compensation levels of the teaching and nursing professions. Social pressures have begun to rectify the compensation problems of teachers. School librarians may benefit from this phenomenon. It is unlikely that academic librarians will feel much impact, particularly in view of the increased attention being given to the costs of higher education in both the public and private sectors.

Our success as a profession depends on the nature and quality of the services we provide and, as it has become increasingly apparent, on cost effectiveness. We should continue to value the nonfinancial rewards of librarianship for, after all, these were the motivation to become members of the profession. But we do the profession and ourselves a disservice if there is no effort made to understand the many factors involved in compensation and utilize these factors to develop appropriate programs.

Compensation programs are based on a number of complex factors internal and external to an organization. These include status and governance, the nature of compensation of faculty and other professionals within the institution, the general cost of living in the area, salary equity and comparable worth considerations, and a variety of other factors, including unionization.

Compensation is many things. It is undoubtedly the most important communication element within an organization. It involves a number of methodologies and philosophies. As Milton Rock (1984) has stated, it is one of the great challenges to management, requiring the creation of "an environment which stimulates people in their jobs" (p. xix).

As important as compensation is in recruiting, maintaining, and motivating staff, it is not the sine qua non in an organization. Job content, developmental opportunities, and performance appraisals are all important parts of the total reward system. In addition, the management style of an organization is becoming an increasingly more important factor in the total reward system. As Rock (1984) has pointed out:

> compensation is more than pay. It is a total reward system involving incentives and noncash benefits, performance appraisal, and work force development as well as base wages and salaries. Thus, in addition to providing for material needs, the compensation administrator must consider the employee's need for self-realization—the need to feel that he or she is having a real impact on the organization. While money, in one form or another, is a major source of satisfaction and motivation, other factors can be equally important to employee morale. These include the nature of the work, the organizational environment and style of management, and the company's past performance and its outlook for the future. (p. xix)

The goal today is to provide an introduction to a complex personnel specialty by outlining the fundamentals for designing and administering a compensation program and reviewing the current issues and problems in compensation management. Although some emphasis will be given to professional positions in academic libraries, the methodologies and philosophies covered are applicable to various types of positions and to various types of libraries.

OBJECTIVES OF COMPENSATION MANAGEMENT

Compensation management is a specialization that developed in business and civil service in response to the growth in the size and complexity of organizations. As a specialization within the personnel area, it is one that gets scant attention in library administration courses. Library directors and library personnel administrators must therefore learn how to deal with compensation as they must learn how to deal with other aspects of library management, whether it be budget planning or fund-raising. Because libraries are part of larger entities, they rely on staff in central administration offices to provide expertise on compensation. This often presents serious disadvantages because of the lack of understanding of the function and duties of academic librarians, a problem compounded by the dramatic changes in academic libraries during the past two decades.

Those who have responsibility for administering compensation programs must educate the specialists in their central personnel offices by presenting them with facts on the nature of library work, particularly that of the professional. The director has an even more important role—i.e., educating the administration of the institution and obtaining funds.

Compensation, stated succinctly, is what employees get in exchange for their work. The adequacy of the compensation has great impact on the ability of an organization to meet its goals. Inadequate compensation leads to poor performance, absenteeism, excessive turnover, grievances, and strikes. Although such problems will never completely disappear, morale can be positively affected if an organization has formulated and disseminated its compensation objectives.

The objectives of compensation programs are quite practical:

1. *Recruitment.* Compensation needs to be competitive to attract qualified applicants. It also needs to respond to the supply and demand of workers.
2. *Retention.* Competitive compensation prevents excessive turnover.
3. *Equity.* Internal equity requires that pay be related to the relative worth of jobs. That is, similar jobs get similar pay. External equity involves paying workers at a rate equal to the pay that similar workers receive in other companies.
4. *Reward desired behavior.* Compensation should reinforce desired behaviors and act as an incentive for those behaviors to occur in the future.
5. *Control costs.* A sound compensation program helps an organization to obtain and retain its work force at a reasonable cost. Without a systematic wage and salary structure the organization could overpay or underpay its employees.
6. *Comply with legal regulations.* As with other aspects of personnel management, wage and salary administration faces legal constraints. A sound pay program considers these constraints and ensures compliance with all government regulations that affect employee compensation.
7. *Further administrative efficiency.* In pursuing the other objectives of effective compensation management, wage and salary specialists try to design the program so that it can be efficiently administered. Administrative efficiency, however, should be a secondary consideration compared with other objectives (Werther & Davis, 1981, p. 318).

JOB EVALUATION OR CLASSIFICATION

To determine what to pay employees in exchange for their work, some method of evaluating or classifying their duties is needed. As O. Glenn Stahl (1962) pointed out, this need was recognized by the U.S. Senate some 150 years ago:

> On the insistence of a number of government clerks urging equal pay for equal work in 1838, the United States Senate was moved to pass a resolution instructing department heads to prepare a "classification of the clerks...in reference to the character of the labor to be performed, the care and responsibility imposed, the qualifications required, and the relative values to the public of the services of each class as compared with the others." (p. 148)

Despite an early recognition of problems in the federal service, Congress did not take comprehensive action to establish classification systems until 1923.

It is the rare exception now to find an organization that does not have some system of organizing positions or functions along with salary schedules outlining compensation levels. In academic libraries, we find a variety of job evaluation systems in effect. The most common are based on systems developed in business and industry, namely, job ranking, job grading, factor comparison, and point systems. Libraries with faculty and academic status often develop ranking systems for professional positions using the model and often the titles of teaching faculty. The Columbia University Libraries developed a system which combines both traditional position classification and faculty ranking systems (Duda, 1980).

The most common job evaluation systems follow systematic procedures to determine the relative value or worth of a position and generally take into consideration skills, responsibilities, experience, and work conditions. They all involve some degree of subjectivity.

Job Ranking. The simplest and least precise method of job evaluation is job ranking. Specialists review the job analysis information. Then each job is ranked subjectively according to its relative importance in comparison with other jobs. These are overall rankings, although raters may consider the responsibility, skill, effort, and working conditions of each job. It is quite possible that important elements of some jobs may be overlooked while unimportant items are weighted too heavily. Even more damaging, these rankings do not differentiate the relative importance between jobs. For example, the job of a janitor may be ranked as 1, the secretary's job may get a 2, and the office manager is ranked 3. But the secretarial position may be three times as important as the janitorial job and half as important as the job of office manager. The job ranking approach does not allow for these relative differences between jobs. Pay scales based on these broad rankings ensure that more important jobs are paid more. But since the rankings lack precision, the resulting pay levels may be inaccurate.

Job Grading. Job grading or job classification is a slightly more sophisticated method than job ranking, though still not very precise. It works by having each job assigned to a grade. The standard description in the figure that most nearly matches the job description determines the grade of the job. Once again, more important jobs are paid more. But the lack of precision can lead to inaccurate pay levels. The largest user of this approach has been the U.S. Civil Service Commission, which gradually is replacing this method with more sophisticated approaches.

Factor Comparison. The factor comparison method requires the job evaluation committee to compare critical job components. The critical components are those factors common to all the jobs being evaluated—such as responsibility, skill, mental effort, physical effort, and working conditions. Each of these factors is compared, one at a time, with the same factor for the other jobs. This evaluation allows the committee to determine the relative importance of each job. The factor comparison method involves the following five steps:

Step 1: Determining the critical factors.

Step 2: Determining key jobs.

Step 3: Apportioning present wages for key jobs.

Step 4: Placing key jobs on a factor comparison.

Step 5: Evaluating benchmark jobs.

Point System. Research shows that the point system is used more than any other method. This system evaluates the critical factors of each job. But instead of using wages, as the factor comparison method does, it uses points. Although more difficult to develop initially, the point system is more precise than the factor comparison method because it can handle critical factors in more detail. This system requires six steps and is usually implemented by a job evaluation committee or by an individual analyst.

Step 1: Determine critical factors.

Step 2: Determine levels of factors.

Step 3: Allocate points to subfactors.

Step 4: Allocate points to levels.

Step 5: Develop the point manual.

Step 6: Apply the point system (Werther & Davis, 1985, pp. 319-26).

As noted earlier, the problem with these systems is subjectivity. In their study of pay equity, Donald Treiman and Heidi Hartman (1981) observed:

> It is important to recognize that job evaluation ultimately rests on judgments. Jobs are described in terms of their tasks, duties, and responsibilities, and these descriptions are rated or ranked with respect to some set of factors. The factor ratings are seldom based on objective information; rather, they represent judgments about such amorphous features of jobs as the responsibility entailed or the experience required. The nature of job evaluation makes it possible for bias to enter at two points: in the writing of the job descriptions and in the evaluation of the descriptions with respect to a set of factors. (p. 77)

Despite the problems inherent in job classification systems, Treiman and Hartman (1981) recognize that job evaluation systems do "provide a systematic method of comparing jobs to determine whether they are fairly compensated" (p. 81). They also recognize the possibility of improving them.

Although the point system method of job evaluation is not void of subjectivity, it is generally considered the most objective. The best known is the Hay System, which was developed by Edward N. Hay and Dale Purves in 1951. It has been applied in some library settings; however, it has not gained wide acceptance in academic librarianship. This may be due to the real or imagined problems academic library administrators see in assigning points to management functions and to the functions of so-called knowledge workers, that is, librarians engaged primarily in collection development, reference, and bibliographic control. Personal experience has demonstrated that this is not necessarily the case. In updating the classification scheme for librarian positions at Columbia in 1985, the professional classification task force recognized certain drawbacks to position-grading systems which "can lead to inequities and to an eventual erosion of the scheme" (Columbia University Libraries, 1985, p. II-17). To compensate for this, a set of principles or point factors were developed to provide "a more consistent approach in the overall assessment of positions" (Columbia University Libraries, 1985, pp. II-17).

The difficulties in evaluating professional and managerial positions are found, as Paul Pigors and Charles Myers (1977) have noted, in all professions:

> [Professional jobs] are much more difficult to describe and analyze in terms of the job content and job factors. Job assignments to many professional people are given on the basis of their individual professional qualifications, and only in large organizations is it possible to describe broad categories of engineering or scientific jobs. This has been called the "generic" approach, which is used in place of either the individual approach or the "career-curve" approach based on professional degrees and years of service. In the latter, the more advanced professional degrees a person has and the longer the service, the higher the salary. Public school teachers are often paid on this basis.
>
> Some authorities believe that managerial positions at the higher levels are difficult to evaluate because the work of the job is so much a function of the individual in it. As one management consultant has said, "It is pointless to talk about evaluating an executive job, when the real evaluation relates to what an individual has made of his job, compared with what others have made of their jobs. In the final analysis, an executive is 'worth' what his superiors believe he is worth. He might have added, "and what other firms might pay him if he left." (p. 368)

The quality and success of a job classification scheme will depend to a large extent on the process used in its design and implementation. Since it is impossible for one person to have all the knowledge and understanding necessary to evaluate all jobs in an organization, a job classification committee can play a critical role in the development of a scheme. The committee should be comprised of appropriate representatives from the organization and conduct its work openly. The latter is particularly important because the more open the scheme is to review by employees whose jobs are affected, the better the likelihood that the scheme will be accepted (Henderson, 1985, pp. 268-69).

DESIGNING A COMPENSATION PROGRAM

The completion or modification of a job classification or evaluation scheme is the first step in designing a compensation program. The authority of the library director in the design and implementation of either job classification schemes or compensation programs will vary considerably, depending on the organizational structure of the institution, the status of the librarians in the institution, and governance. The authority of directors in libraries with collective bargaining agreements and those in the public sector is often limited, and they may face seemingly insurmountable obstacles in both classification and compensation. Academic library directors in private institutions, on the other hand, often have considerable discretion in these areas.

Regardless of local constraints, directors have the most important role to play in establishing and modifying compensation programs. As chief administrators of the library, they are responsible for meeting the service objectives of the institution. Their success in this effort will depend on their ability to recruit, motivate, and retain high quality staff. They should rely on their library personnel administrators to provide the data and expertise to support their arguments, but they must also understand the dimensions of salary compensation and the factors common to all organizations and to libraries specifically.

Common Organizational Factors

There are a number of factors common to all organizations that should be considered carefully in any effort to design or modify a compensation program (Pigors & Myers, 1977):

1. the quality of employees the organization needs for effective operation,
2. the competition of other organizations for employees of this quality; and
3. the ability of the organization to pay levels of wages and salaries that will attract and hold the people it needs (pp. 334-35).

Internal Differences

An important initial step in designing or modifying a salary program involves a review of existing policy, both institutional and library. Institutional policies generally include the following factors:

1. Minimum and maximum levels of pay (taking into consideration ability and willingness to pay, government regulations, union influences, and market pressures).
2. The general relationships among levels of pay (between nonexempt and exempt senior management and operating management, operatives, and supervisors).
3. The division of the total compensation dollar (i.e., what portion goes into base pay, what portion into benefits, what portion into merit pay or pay-for-performance programs) (Henderson, 1985, p. 379).

Within these general guidelines, the following determinations then have to be made:

1. What is the lowest rate of pay that can be offered for a job that will entice the quality of employees the organization desires to have as its members?
2. What is the rate of pay that must be offered to incumbents to ensure that they remain with the organization?
3. Is it wise or necessary to offer more than one rate of pay to employees performing either identical or similar work?
4. What is considered to be a sufficient difference in base rates of pay among jobs in a class series that require varying levels or knowledge and skills and responsibilities and duties?
5. Does the organization wish to recognize dangerous and distressing working conditions within the base pay schedule?

6. Should there be a difference in changes in base pay progression opportunities among jobs of varying worth?
7. Do employees have a significant opportunity to profess to higher-level jobs? If so, what should be the relationship between promotion to a higher job and changes in base pay?
8. Will policies and regulations permit incumbents to earn rates of pay higher than established maximums and lower than established minimums? What would be the reasons for allowing such deviations?
9. How will the pay structure accommodate across-the-board, cost of living or other adjustments not related to employee tenure, performance, or responsibility and duty changes (Henderson, 1985, pp. 379-80)?

Salary Surveys

Salary surveys are considered an essential step in designing or modifying a salary program. They involve several steps:

1. *Selection of area or industry, and firms or organizations to be included in the survey.* This is frequently a point of difference with unions since the inclusion of low-wage, nonunion firms in the sample will usually cause a particular firm's wage level to compare "favorably" with the community or industry.
2. *Listing key jobs and positions common to most firms in the survey.* Detailed descriptions of these jobs [are needed], so that valid comparisons can be made.
3. *Making a schedule of information to be obtained*, e.g., hourly rates or earnings, weekly earnings or salaries, hours worked, shift premiums, other wage and salary supplements, and methods of wage payment. These data are necessary since the meaning of "wages" and "salaries" often varies in different organizations.
4. *Collection of accurate wage and salary data* on jobs that are essentially similar, by questionnaires, or preferably interviews, in each firm.
5. *Compilation of the wage and salary data for each job*, showing the mean or arithmetical average, the median, the range of rates paid, and supplementary wage and salary data. The data may also be reported by companies or organizations, labeled *A, B, C*, etc.
6. *Finally, presentation of results and recommendations* to management (Pigors & Myers, 1977, pp. 335-36).

Salary surveys may be taken before or during the actual design of a salary structure and are generally considered the most helpful tools in compensation management. They should not be undertaken without thorough review of survey techniques and methodology.

A critical aspect of any salary survey is identifying key or benchmark positions. Simply identifying job keys by title does not provide sufficient information. For example, the scope of responsibilities of an interlibrary loan librarian may vary considerably from one library to another. To avoid this pitfall a job summary should be developed. This should consist of a clear summary of the job description, which provides information on both the general and specific responsibilities of the position (Henderson, 1985, p. 343).

Fortunately, the library profession has access to important salary data. For many years academic librarians have relied on the annual salary surveys of the Association of Research Libraries which in recent years has been expanded to provide data on ranks and minority status. Another important source of data is the *ALA Survey of Librarian Salaries,* first published in 1982 and expanded in 1984 to include members of the Association of Research Libraries.

There are a variety of informal regional salary surveys in academic librarianship such as those conducted by the Big Ten, the Gnomes (Chicago, Columbia, Cornell, Harvard, M.I.T., Princeton, Stanford, Yale), and the ACRL Personnel Officers Discussion Group. In addition, libraries interested in salary information on specific specialist positions can contract with ARL for the manipulation of their database.

Mechanics of Designing a Compensation Program

Both job classification and salary surveys involve a number of complexities that cannot be mastered without considerable study and the expertise of specialists. Neither can be approached without careful consideration of institutional policies and guidelines. There is much at stake here because the final product carries great weight. It tells employees what value the organization places on jobs, the job and compensation advancement opportunities available, and how competitive the pay practices are with other organizations.

Although librarians might seem to be at a disadvantage when faced with the technical aspects of compensation design, the fact that academic libraries are components of larger institutions or governmental bodies means that compensation specialists should be available to provide the necessary expertise. A brief summary of some of the technical aspects involved in designing a pay structure provides an indication of the complexity involved.

1. *Determining a pay policy line.* A pay policy line is one that best represents the middle pay value of jobs that have been evaluated or classified to have particular worth. It is arrived at through various mathematical formulas.
2. *Deciding on the need for more than one pay structure.* Since there are different forces at play for different occupational groups, different pay structures are required for, for example, clerical workers, unskilled workers, and professionals and administrators.
3. *Identifying lowest and highest rates of pay.* Consideration here must be given to legal issues, such as the Fair Labor Standards Act as well as to the ability of the organization to pay.

4. *Developing pay grades.* Pay grades are basically convenient group-
   ings of a wide variety of jobs or classes similar in work difficulty and
   responsibility requirements. They provide a link between the evaluation and classification process and the assignment of pay to a particular job or class (Henderson, 1985, p. 343).

   After the technical aspects of design have been completed, compensation experts need to review the program to ensure that there is an
orderly and logical progression in the structure. This is necessary to
ensure that:

1. All jobs have been analyzed and described.
2. Jobs have either been classified or evaluated so that an internally
   equitable ordering of jobs can be established.
3. Jobs have been located on a scatter diagram and clusters of jobs have
   been identified so that a first attempt can be made at a potentially
   acceptable grouping of jobs for classification or grading purposes.
4. One or more benchmark (key) jobs have been identified for each
   potential pay grade.
5. A survey has been completed in which actual rates of pay and pay
   range data have been collected. (This is a huge assumption as many
   surveys are not designed to collect actual rate of pay.)
6. Pay survey data have been analyzed and a summary of the data
   includes mean and median (50th percentile) rates of pay for each job;
   10th, 25th, 75th, and 90th percentile data; lowest and highest rates of
   pay reported for each job; average established range maximums and
   minimums for each job; and highest maximum and lowest minimum or reported established ranges (Henderson, 1985, pp. 418-19).

EXTERNAL INFLUENCES ON COMPENSATION

Government Influences

The British Parliament passed a minimum wage act in 1562 (Henderson, 1985, p. 64), but it was not until several hundred years after the
beginning of the Industrial Revolution that society began recognizing
the inhumane aspects of working conditions. Although President Martin Van Buren issued an executive order establishing a 10-hour day for
workers on government contracts in 1840, it was not until after the Civil
War that efforts began to reduce working hours and increase wages in
the United States (Henderson, 1985, p. 65). Modern legislation dealing
with employment and compensation began in the 1930s. The major acts
relating to compensation practices may be categorized under the broad
headings of wage and hour legislation, income protection legislation,
and antidiscrimination legislation (Henderson, 1985, pp. 67-68).

Wage and Hour Legislation. The *Davis-Bacon Act* of 1931 was the
first national legislation on minimum wages. It required construction
contractors and subcontractors receiving federal funds in excess of
$2,000 to pay at least the prevailing wages in the area.

The *National Industrial Recovery Act* (NIRA) of 1933 was an attempt to establish a national minimum wage. It was declared unconstitutional by the U.S. Supreme Court in 1935.

The *National Labor Relations Act* of 1935 gave employees the right to bargain collectively for wages, benefits, and working conditions.

The *Walsh-Healy Public Contracts Act* of 1936 was another attempt of the federal government to deal with minimum wages. It required that prevailing wages be paid in all government-sponsored contract work exceeding $10,000 and time-and-a-half for work exceeding eight hours a day and forty hours a week.

The *Fair Labor Standards Act* (FLSA) of 1938 enabled the "federal government to become deeply involved in regulating minimum wages for all employees engaged in interstate or foreign commerce or in the production of goods for such commerce, and for all employees in certain enterprises" (Henderson, 1985, p. 68). It also established wage requirements and defined specific occupations. The Fair Labor Standards Act, as amended, has had considerable impact on wages and hours, including the establishment of the minimum hourly rate.

Income Protection Legislation. Both federal and state governments have become increasingly involved in providing economic protection for the compensation of employees beginning with the enactment of Worker's Compensation in 1911 (Henderson, 1985, pp. 71-79). Other landmark laws enacted are the Social Security Act of 1935 and Unemployment Compensation (Title IX of the Social Security Act of 1935).

Laws relating to pensions are the most recent in the income protection area. The primary ones are the Welfare and Pension Plan Disclosure Act of 1959 and the Employee Retirement Income Security Act (ERISA) of 1974.

Antidiscrimination Legislation and Compensation. Starting in the 1960s, a number of laws and executive orders, based on the Bill of Rights, have been passed that have brought civil rights into the workplace. Those relating most directly to compensation are:

The *Equal Pay Act* of 1963, an amendment to the Fair Labor Standards Act. It is the first federal antidiscrimination law relating directly to women. It requires equal pay for equal work for men and women, defining equal work as that which requires equal skill, effort, and responsibility under similar working conditions. Under the Equal Pay Act, employers can only establish different wage rates on the basis of (1) a seniority system, (2) a merit system, and (3) a differential based on any factor other than sex. All such exemptions must apply equally to men and women (Henderson, 1985, p. 80).

Title VII of the Civil Rights Act of 1964, known also as the Equal Opportunity Employment Act. It prohibits unlawful employment practices including failure to hire, failure to provide employment, or failure to promote because of a person's race, color, religion, sex, or national origin (Henderson, 1985, p. 81).

Equal Pay and Comparable Worth. The concept of "equal pay for work of comparable value" is commonly known as "comparable worth" and "pay equity." Although the terms are sometimes used interchangeably, there are important distinctions. Both the Equal Pay Act and Title VII address discrimination in compensation which is why both acts are considered in cases involving sex discrimination in compensation.

Title VII came into play in discrimination cases because the Equal Pay Act is limited to situations in which men and women do the same or similar work as described in the standards of the act, namely, that the jobs require equal skill, effort, and responsibility. Although the standard for comparing jobs is the same under Title VII as under the Equal Pay Act, the prohibition against discrimination in compensation in Title VII is stated more broadly than in the Equal Pay Act, implying that there may be a broader base of recovery under Title VII. For example:

> An individual seeking to redress sex-based wage differentials under the Equal Pay Act must demonstrate that persons of the opposite sex working for the same single establishment are paid higher wages for substantially equal work. Title VII, however, does not contain a "single establishment" requirement. In a Title VII sex-based wage discrimination suit, a bias claimant may properly present to the court evidence that employees of the opposite sex working at separate establishments maintained by the employer receive higher wages for substantially equal work. (Commerce Clearing House, 1986, p. 25)

Comparable worth is fundamentally an approach to expanding coverage of sex discrimination in compensation under Title VII of the Civil Rights Act of 1964. Although there have been more than 100 state and local government initiatives on comparable worth since the late 1970s, no federal legislation has been enacted which identifies and defines a method for determining comparable worth. Recent initiatives dealing with equal pay and comparable worth range from a pay equity study in New York State to the appropriation in Minnesota of $21.7 million in the spring of 1983 for pay equity increases over a two-year period. (In the spring of 1985, the Minnesota legislature allocated an additional $11.7 million to complete pay equity implementation for state employees by 1987 [ALA, 1987].)

Treiman and Hartman (1981) recognize that there are no simple answers to the questions raised by comparable worth. They are convinced, however, that bias does exist:

> Our economy is structured so that some jobs will inevitably pay less than others, and the fact that many such jobs are disproportionately filled by women and minorities may reflect differences in qualifications, interests, traditional roles, and similar factors; or it may reflect exclusionary practices with regard to hiring and promotion; or it may reflect a combination of both. However, several types of evidence support our judgment that it is also true in many instances that jobs held mainly by women and minorities pay less at least in part *because* they are held mainly by women and minorities. First, the differentials in average pay for jobs held mainly by women and those held mainly by men persists when the characteristics of jobs thought to affect their

value and the characteristics of workers thought to affect their productivity are held constant. Second, prior to the legislation of the past two decades, differentials in pay for men and women and for minorities and nonminorities were often acceptable and were, in fact, prevalent. The tradition embodied in such practices was built into wage structures, and its effects continue to influence these structures. Finally, at the level of the specific firm, several studies show that women's jobs are paid less on the average than men's jobs with the same scores derived from job evaluation plans. The evidence is not complete or conclusive, but the consistency of the results in many different job categories and in several different types of studies, the size of the pay differentials (even after worker and job characteristics have been taken into account) and the lack of evidence for alternative explanations strongly suggest that wage discrimination is widespread. (p. 93)

It is clear that equal pay and comparable worth issues will be the primary area of focus in compensation for some time. In view of the different approaches underway in states such as Minnesota, California, and Washington, it seems that a variety of different methods will be used to resolve salary inequities (Treiman & Hartmann, 1981, pp. 69-90; ALA, 1987).

The American Library Association

The American Library Association, which represents a profession dominated by women, has been active in supporting the concepts of equal pay and comparable worth and is represented on the board of directors of the National Committee on Pay Equity. Through its Office for Library Personnel Resources, ALA provides a variety of information sources on pay equity and is committed to educating members through programs such as the pay equity institute held at its annual conference in 1986 (ALA, 1987). ALA's Office of Library Personnel Resources recently announced plans to develop a casebook that would help library workers document discrepancies and work toward establishing pay equity.

The Influence of Unions

Although there has been a decline in union influence since the 1970s, unions continue to have a strong influence on compensation. Moreover, minorities and women are becoming more active in the union movement, which makes issues of equal pay and comparable worth of particular interest in organizing campaigns and collective bargaining. Unions were in the forefront in making progress in, for example, Connecticut, Washington, and Minnesota. They will continue to be actively involved in issues of equal pay and comparable worth.

MERIT OR PERFORMANCE-BASED REWARD SYSTEMS

Financial incentive systems supplement salary and should be addressed in the design of a compensation program (Werther & Davis, 1985). A variety of incentive systems are common in business and industry—production bonuses, profit-sharing, incentive programs, commissions—but are not relevant in the academic library environment. Others, such as overtime and shift differentials, generally apply only to individuals in nonexempt classifications.

Merit Systems

The most common financial incentive system found in academic libraries is merit, often referred to in business and industry as "performance-based reward programs." Merit systems are found in a variety of academic libraries, including those covered by collective bargaining agreements and civil service. There is a great variety in merit pay programs and each organization should consider the variables that apply to its situation when designing or implementing such a program. Among the variables that are particularly applicable to libraries are:

1. ability to specify quality and quantity of good service;
2. employee needs, perceptions, and demands; and
3. external environmental pressures, including consumers of goods or services, market demand for goods or services, legal requirements, and society in general (Henderson, 1985, p. 488).

The Equal Pay Act permits employers to administer merit raises without concern that a differential that may result can be found to be unlawful under the act (Commerce Clearing House, 1986, p. 20).

Performance Standards

The success of a merit system will depend to a great degree on standards which will be scrutinized and analyzed by those affected. All work-related standards, whether they apply to evaluating jobs, establishing pay rates, or assessing work performance, should meet two criteria:

1. *Consistency.* Standards must be consistent; that is, a standard must recognize similar employee inputs by providing similar employer output. (If job knowledge, responsibility requirements, and working conditions are similar, base rates should likewise be similar. Similar work effort by employees having similar skills and motivation should result in comparable piecerate earnings or performance appraisal ratings.)
2. *Fairness.* Standards must be fair. Whatever the final purpose of the standard, those persons working under its rules must accept it as just and reasonable (Henderson, 1985, p. 489).

A major problem with performance standards is, of course, interpretation. Individual biases in the form of differing expectations come into play which require continual discussion and review to ensure equity and consistent application. Normally the responsibility for interpreting and assessing performance standards rests with management, the chief administrator, and the personnel administrator. The personnel administrator, however, should not have the final say in such matters.

Performance Appraisal Programs

Implicit in any merit system is an ongoing performance appraisal program which may be similar or different from the program used for merit raises. In addition to their function in merit, performance appraisals are important in promotional opportunities within an organization and in identifying developmental opportunities for future advancement. As such, they are an integral aspect of an organization's compensation program.

Responsibility for Merit Adjustments

Line management clearly has responsibility for getting effective results and should be concerned with the wages and salaries paid to those they supervise. Personnel administrators have an important function to perform in the development, implementation, and interpretation of performance standards; but they should not overrule the line. Any disputes between the personnel administrator and a line manager should be referred to the head librarian who can resolve the matter with the appropriate senior administrator.

BENEFITS AND SERVICES

Fringe benefits are an important part of any compensation program and have been the focus of considerable attention in the 1980s because of increased employee needs and the escalation of costs to the employer. It is not uncommon to find employers cutting back on fringe benefits, eliminating some programs completely, or requiring employees to carry a portion of the cost.

It is not uncommon to find that 35 percent of payroll costs—that is, an additional 35 percent of an employee's annual salary—are allocated to benefits. It is predicted that this figure will increase to 50 percent by 1990 (Henderson, 1985, p. 432).

There are five reasons given to explain the spiraling cost of benefits in the past forty years:

1. The imposition of wage ceilings during World War II forced organizations to offer more and greater benefits in place of wage increases to attract new employees and to keep current workers.
2. With the increasing unacceptability of autocratic management and the decline of paternalism, instead of using threats or a variety of protective procedures, organizations have used benefits to gain employee compliance and loyalty, which has resulted in a more acceptable form of paternalism.
3. Possibly the most important reason for the increases has been the rise of union influence and the steady increase of wages to the point where they now satisfy the basic needs of the employees they represent. In turn, this has led to increased interest and bargaining for more and greater benefits.

4. In the 1970s, inflation, rising wage levels, and heavier income tax burdens aroused increased interest in tax shelters at lower levels in the organizational structure. Many employers are now providing an even greater array of benefits than employees consider valuable. This approach reduces the tax burden of the employer and, at the same time, increases the disposable income available to employees by providing benefits and services they would otherwise have to purchase with after tax dollars.

5. More recent changes in public policy to shift the cost burden from the federal government to private sector employers regarding health care services and protection and continuing public concern over the long-term viability of social security have placed even greater pressure on employers to provide more protection in these already costly areas (Henderson, 1985, pp. 432-33).

We will continue to see efforts to restrict the percentage of the payroll that goes to benefits. Many institutions and organizations have recognized the need for cost containment and have either renegotiated their benefits coverage with their usual carriers or contracted with new carriers. The advent of employee spending accounts and flexible benefit plans are the results of efforts of the federal government to bring the rapidly escalating costs of benefits under control.

We usually consider benefits as components of the compensation program that provide protection in case of health-related problems and income at some future date, such as upon retirement or termination of employment. Employee services, which vary greatly, are also part of the total compensation program. The two major elements of employee services are (1) pay for time not worked—holidays, vacation, jury duty; and (2) income equivalent payments (education subsidies, child-care, subsidized housing) and reimbursements for incurred expenses (moving expenses, travel reimbursement).

Although benefits and services are sometimes viewed as the forgotten stepchild of the total compensation package, they have become increasingly more important in the recruitment and retention of staff. They are complicated because of the variety of components and options available, legal requirements, and financial implications. Although benefits present many complexities, it is incumbent upon compensation and personnel administrators to develop a fundamental understanding of benefits so that they can work with the specialists in efforts to provide the best coverage for available dollars.

COMPENSATION ADMINISTRATION

Timely and Proper Administration

A compensation program is not complete until procedures and processes are in place to ensure timely and proper administration. This includes taking steps to ensure that employees understand the nature of the program. Employees should not have to search for answers to such basic questions as:

1. When is the next pay day?
2. When is the first increase possible?
3. What are the criteria for raises?
4. What are the eligibility requirements for vacations?
5. How long is the first vacation?
6. How many paid holidays are there? What are they? Are there eligibility requirements?
7. What are the criteria for promotions?
8. Are cost-of-living adjustments provided?
9. How are overtime opportunities determined?
10. Is an employee's pay ever reduced (Henderson, 1985, p. 582)?

A great amount of time and money is expended in developing or modifying a compensation program. Its success should not be endangered by a failure to apprise employees of the nature of the program or to take steps to ensure that all payroll transactions are processed in a timely fashion. The latter is often the major flaw in salary administration. Delays in processing payroll transactions can seriously damage the credibility of the personnel office. Regardless of where the snags develop—within the library or in some central institutional office—the library personnel staff should resolve the problem.

Pay Structure Adjustments

Most organizations make annual adjustments to the structure of their salary program. In organizations covered by collective bargaining agreements or civil service, the adjustments are often known several years in advance, and the function of the library personnel administrator is limited to processing payroll adjustments. In organizations where there is more flexibility, it is not uncommon for library directors to take an active part in determining changes in the salary structure, particularly in the program for professional librarians.

Merit Guidelines

When merit increases are a part of a salary program, many libraries follow guidelines to determine adjustments and to assure that salary differentials are based on demonstrated performance. Although merit guidelines vary, they have certain basic characteristics.

—*Maximum:* Performs in a superior manner for sustained period of time ("superior" or "distinguished"). Performs in a commendable manner; consistently exceeds fully satisfactory levels of performance for extended periods of time ("commendable" or "fully satisfactory").
—*Midpoint:* Consistently performs all responsibilities in a fully satisfactory manner; is fully trained and normally has from 2 to 4 years of experience on the job ("satisfactory" or "competent"). Performs

responsibilities between a marginal and a satisfactory level. Incumbent is still in a learning stage and has not performed all responsibilities at a fully proficient level for a reasonable period (e.g., 6 months).

—*Minimum:* Performs responsibilities at a marginal or less level. If in this pay bracket for more than 24 months, should be assigned or terminated ("unacceptable"). Probationary range (Henderson, 1985, p. 595).

Words like "distinguished," "superior," and "competent" are loaded and have different meanings to different people which is why they are in quotation marks. In some organizations, descriptive terms are avoided.

Merit Pay Distribution Schedules

Certain aspects of merit pay distribution seem particularly appealing in the academic environment because of the constraints of available funds. These include a policy for paying different rates of pay to individuals receiving identical merit ratings (Henderson, 1985, p. 596). This generally means that individuals in the upper ranges receive a smaller percentage increase than those in the lower ranges. It is an effective way of rewarding and encouraging less senior staff members.

Forced-distribution rating systems are sometimes used, which require distributing percentage increases according to a predetermined mix which includes limiting the number of superior ratings (Henderson, 1985, pp. 594-96). Forced distribution systems present certain psychological constraints and can create inequities and morale problems if applied too narrowly.

Merit pay distribution schedules based on actual percentages, on the other hand, can be helpful tools in budget planning. The following is an example of such a schedule (Henderson, 1985, p. 596):

MERIT PAY DISTRIBUTION SCHEDULE
(based on actual percentages)

Performance Rating	Distribution	Merit Range Increase
Superior	Top 5 to 10%	10 to 20%
Commendable	Next 10 to 15%	8 to 12%
Satisfactory	Middle 60 to 75%	6 to 10%
Marginal	Next 5 to 10%	0 to 5%
Unacceptable	Bottom 0 to 5%	0%

If there is a relatively consistent interpretation of performance standards in an organization, the distribution schedule often remains relatively the same over several years, although the specific individuals within the distribution will vary.

Other Compensation Administration Issues

There are many other aspects of compensation administration and some mention should be made of several because of their importance to the overall program.

Pay Plan Analysis. Compa-ratio is one method of analysis which enables management to assess a compensation program (Henderson, 1985, pp. 603-04). It involves an analysis of pay grades or salary ranges which cannot be done unless midpoints are set and jobs are assigned to pay grades. The compa-ratio enables an organization to determine its competitiveness and can be used to analyze the pay treatment of specific groups of employees by such factors as gender, race, or age group.

Guidelines for Promotion and Demotion. There is wide variation in policies on promotion and demotion. To ensure equity it is important to have written guidelines.

Premium Rates and Market Considerations. Major problems for compensation administrators occur when there is a considerable shortage of workers with particular knowledge or skill (e.g., computer specialists). To prevent inequities, these special situations should be recognized in both the classification and compensation systems. Equally problematic are efforts to accommodate so-called "superstars." Such practices are not uncommon in academia, where institutions make a variety of concessions, including compensation, to attract star teaching and research staff. In academic librarianship such negotiations generally only take place with individuals negotiating for directorships.

The Computer and Compensation

Payroll was one of the earliest processes to benefit from computerization, and automated personnel information systems now provide a vast variety of information on payroll, benefits, and other elements of compensation. Libraries often find a need for information not always readily available from the institution's personnel information system. The advent of personal computers with an array of spreadsheet and database systems available at reasonable costs enables the staff in the library personnel office to supplement the institutions' system to meet specific library needs in areas as diverse as budget planning and administration and monitoring performance appraisal schedules and applicant flow data.

RESPONSIBILITIES IN COMPENSATION MANAGEMENT

Line managers have considerable responsibility for accomplishing organizational objectives and should therefore have an appropriate role in compensation management. Their influence in this important area may be quite limited in institutions in the public sector and in those covered by collective bargaining agreements. Regardless of the constraints within the organization, however, senior level administrators and line managers should not be passive observers in the various components that form the basis of an institution's compensation program. The personnel department has an important role to play in compensation administration, but it does not and should not have all the power and the final say in developing, modifying, and administering the program.

The improvement of organizations and institutions is a major challenge of contemporary society. Personnel administrators have an important contribution to make in meeting this challenge. Directors and managers in academic libraries often rely on personnel administrators to resolve problems involving the human resources in the organization in many areas, including compensation. Personnel administrators have a key role in an organization, but that role must be viewed in perspective.

A brief review of contemporary viewpoints of personnel management can help place it in a proper perspective:

1. *Human resource approach.* Personnel management is the management of human resources. The importance and dignity of human beings should not be ignored for the sake of expediency. Only through careful attention to the needs of employees do successful organizations grow and prosper.
2. *Management approach.* Personnel management is the responsibility of every manager. The personnel department exists to serve managers and employees through its expertise. So, in the final analysis, the performance and well-being of each worker is the dual responsibility of that worker's immediate supervisor and the personnel department.
3. *Systems approach.* Personnel management takes place within a larger system: the organization. Therefore, personnel management must be evaluated with respect to the contribution it makes to the organization's productivity. In practice, experts must recognize that the personnel management model is an open system of interrelated parts. Each part affects the others and is influenced by the external environment.
4. *Proactive approach.* Personnel management can increase its contribution to employees, managers, and the organization by anticipating challenges before they arise. If efforts are reactive only, problems may be compounded and opportunities may be missed (Werther & Davis, 1985, p. 25).

Implicit in all these viewpoints is the limited role of personnel administrators. They play a critical role as resources to their directors, but it is the directors who carry the final responsibility for developing or modifying compensation programs not only for professionals but for all members of the library staff.

Appendix A

Developing Compensation Systems in Academic Libraries
Exercise: Salary Equity Analysis (Columbia University, 1978)

Background

As part of its affirmative action analysis for the federal government, University X is required to undertake a salary equity analysis to determine whether, and the extent to which, women and minorities have been subjected to salary discrimination by reason of their sex or ethnicity. With respect to professional librarians, the examination will be conducted through a four-step analysis.

Step 1: Determination of Counterparts

The analysis will begin by identifying, for each female and minority person, one or more white male counterparts, determined on the basis of objective factors to be developed in consultation with the university librarian. If one or more of the males match the female or minority person with respect to all of the objective factors, those white males will be considered counterparts of the female or minority person.

The librarians at University X are not unionized and have academic status. The counterparts for librarians are determined initially by rank:
Librarian Instructor (Rank I)
Assistant Librarian (Rank II)
Associate Librarian (Rank III)
Librarian (Rank IV)

Step 2: Mechanical Screening

The salary, as of May 1, 1987, of the female or minority person (averaged with the salaries of other female or minority persons who are also counterparts, if any) will be compared with the mean (average) and the median of the white male counterparts. If it is more than 5 percent below either, the case will be considered a situation that warrants further scrutiny and will be analyzed in detail under step 3. If there is no counterpart for the female or minority person, no further analysis will be conducted.

Step 3: Analysis of Nondiscriminatory Factors

Every case identified for further scrutiny will first be examined to determine whether that person's relative salary position is attributable to certain nondiscriminatory factors which will be examined for their relative impact. Where discrepancies remain unexplained by objective factors, the analysis will turn to judgmental factors. Throughout this analysis, differences of 5 percent or less will be considered *de minimis*.

Step 4: Determination of Appropriate Salary Adjustments

Where a salary discrepancy is not fully explained by the analysis of factors in step 3, each situation will be reviewed to determine an appropriate salary in light of the analysis in steps 2 and 3. A salary adjustment will be made after consultation with the appropriate dean or other administrative officer.

Committee Assignment

You have been appointed by the university librarian to a committee to recommend relevant factors to be considered in the salary equity analysis for professional librarians. Your specific assignment involves:

1. Identifying nondiscriminatory objective factors that justify a salary differential among counterparts.
2. Identifying nondiscriminatory judgmental factors that justify a salary differential among counterparts (Columbia University, 1978).

REFERENCES

American Library Association. (1987). *History of pay equity in Minnesota* (TIP Kit No. 9). Chicago: ALA, Office for Library Personnel Resources.

Brandeis, L. (1914). *Business: A profession.* Boston, MA: Small, Maynard, & Company.

Columbia University Libraries. (1985). The system of professional position categories. In *Handbook for librarians* (pp. II-9-12). Professional Classification Task Force. November 18.

Columbia University. (1978). *Salary equity analysis,* internal documents, August 4.

Commerce Clearing House. (1986). *Harassment and pay discrimination in the work place.* CCH Editorial Staff Publication. Chicago: Commerce Clearing House.

Duda, F. (1980). Columbia's two-track system. *College & Research Libraries, 41*(July), 295-304.

Henderson, R. I. (1985). *Compensation management: Rewarding performance* (4th ed.). Reston, VA: Reston Publishing.

Pigors, P., & Myers, C. A. (1977). *Personnel administration: A point of view and a method* (8th ed.). New York: McGraw-Hill.

Rock, M. L. (Ed.). (1984). *Handbook of wage and salary administration* (2nd ed.). New York: McGraw-Hill.

Stahl, G. O. (1962). *Public personnel administration* (5th ed.). New York: Harper & Row.

Treiman, D. J., & Hartman, H. I. (Eds.). (1981). *Women work and wages: Equal pay for jobs of equal value.* Report of the Commission on Occupational Classification and Analysis, National Research Council, National Academy of Sciences. Washington, DC: Academy Press.

Werther, W. B., & Davis, K. (1985). *Personnel management and human resources* (2nd ed.). New York: McGraw-Hill.

ADDITIONAL REFERENCES

American Library Association. (1986). Office of Library Personnel Resources T.I.P. Kit #9 (Topics in Personnel), *Pay Equity: A Selected Bibliography.* May. Mimeographed.

Creth, S. (1981). Personnel planning and utilisation. In S. D. Creth & F. Duda (Eds.), *Personnel Administration in libraries.* New York: Neal Schuman. pp. 57-93.

Duda, F. (1980). Columbia's two-track system. *College & Research Libraries, 41*(July), 295-304.

Lynch, M. J. (1986). ALA salary survey 1986: Figures managers need for setting competitive salaries. *American Libraries, 17*(October), 680.

Treiman, D. J. (1979). *Job evaluation: An analytic review.* Interim report to the Equal Employment Opportunities Commission. Committee on Occupational Classification and Analysis, Assembly of Behavioral and Social Sciences, National Research Council. Washington, DC: National Academy of Sciences Press.

CHRISTOPHER F. BOWEN

Assistant Library Director
Downers Grove Public Library
Downers Grove, Illinois

Developing a Compensation System: The Experience of the Downers Grove Public Library

ABSTRACT

This article uses the experience of one medium-sized public library to survey the steps that might be followed in evaluating an institution, examine the work of its employees, and develop a program to provide equitable compensation to staff at all levels. Consideration is given to analyzing the work of individual employees, creating job descriptions, ranking positions, developing the salary schedule, and maintaining the system.

INTRODUCTION

On March 12, 1985, the Downers Grove Public Library Board of Trustees approved a new compensation system for the library. The development of a new compensation system was undertaken in response to the dramatic changes that took place in the organization during a period of rapid growth in library use, size, and staff.

In the ten years from fiscal year 1976/77 to fiscal year 1984/85, the library grew from a 7,000 square foot facility with thirty-five employees and an annual circulation of 346,000 items, to a 38,000 square foot facility with a staff of seventy-five, circulating 650,000 items per year. This period of growth also included the addition of an automated circulation system and patron access catalog, automated acquisition and cataloging systems, and the division of public services into three separate departments. All of these changes required the staff to learn a variety of skills and assume responsibilities that simply were not recognized in the old system. An examination of the development of the new compensation system provides a general overview of the process of

127

creating any compensation system and also serves as a practical guide to the development of a compensation system for a medium-sized public library.

The first step in developing a new compensation system for an organization is to determine the goals of the project. In his classic work *Compensation,* Robert Sibson (1981) lists six goals for a compensation program: solve pay problems, help attract and retain needed personnel, reward excellence, facilitate communication, support achievement of company objectives, and contribute to organizational development. The Downers Grove Library addressed all these goals in the process of creating a new compensation program.

Fairness in compensating employees was the overall concern of the Downers Grove project. Current management theory states that money is not the prime motivator for good job performance but is chiefly a demotivator. According to Peter Drucker (1954): "Financial rewards and incentives are, of course, important, but they work largely negatively. Discontent with financial rewards is a powerful disincentive, undermining and corroding responsibility for performance" (p. 303). Library employees in particular, while often amazingly dedicated to their work, have always been underpaid, but they do want to be paid equitably with respect to their co-workers (Wheeler & Goldhor, 1981, pp. 88-89). A library clerk may wish to be paid more than $4 per hour, but will still do good work. However, if it is discovered that another employee, doing the same work and with the same seniority earns $4.25 per hour, the employee will feel cheated and productivity will suffer. The three areas specifically targeted for attention in the project all dealt with this issue of fairness.

Before the compensation project the library had only four job classifications—page, clerk, library assistant, and professional. These four classes of jobs did not provide enough distinction in levels of pay or job classification to recognize and compensate the different kinds of tasks performed by library staff. Nor did these classifications provide staff with paths for career advancement. Lack of job descriptions made it difficult for motivated employees to know how to prepare themselves for other positions within the library.

And finally, the starting pay for most staff was too low. However, as there were no ceilings on pay, a few long-time employees earned hourly wages far above the market rate.

The board of trustees wanted a compensation system that would differentiate between positions and allow the library to pay employees more fairly for the work performed, a plan that would make budget planning more efficient by providing definite pay ranges with minimum and maximum pay at each level, a system that could be evaluated and revised easily as needed, and a plan that would facilitate the rewarding of good performance. The board also wanted to examine salaries paid by other area libraries. They decided from the outset that they wanted to break out of the rut of always trying to catch up to the salaries offered by same-sized libraries, and instead offer salaries that were competitive.

CONSULTANT OR DO IT YOURSELF?

Once the decision was made to undertake the project, the first big decision of the project was whether to hire a consultant or do the project in-house. After a considerable amount of research into planning compensation systems, the administration of the library decided to do the project in-house.

The main reason for deciding to do the project in-house rather than hiring a consultant was the issue of control. A consulting firm normally uses its own standard system for evaluating a client's organization. This means that the consultant will often force the organization to fit the consultant's measures rather than developing tools that best fit the client's specific needs and priorities.

For example, another suburban library was included in an organizational analysis of its village government. That library's staff was quite concerned that the criteria used to evaluate the library positions were not relevant to much of the work of a library, although the measures appeared perfectly suited for evaluation of the village government employees.

With the decision to do the project in-house, it was then decided that the administrative team (the library director and the assistant librarian) would head the project, involving other staff wherever possible. The brunt of the work would fall on the administrative team, in part because they were the only library employees with time available to carry out the project since they were not regularly involved in direct public service or support services. Once work began, most of the administrators' time for the next three months was devoted to the project.

Since the structure of the Downers Grove Public Library had changed so dramatically over the years, the project was a perfect opportunity to not only look closely at the work that was being done by the library staff, but to consider whether or not this was still the most effective distribution of the work of the organization. This reevaluation of the organization is a step that is often skipped in developing a new compensation system. Organizations often create a new system that catalogs all the work done by the organization's employees without ever considering whether that work is still appropriate or efficiently distributed. The library administration, by actually being involved in the project, had a golden opportunity to fine-tune the structure of the organization to fit the current goals and priorities of the library.

Further, by doing the project in-house, the library had the opportunity to involve the staff in the process and, as the project proceeded, ensure that the staff was informed of what was happening. The administrative team believed that staff acceptance of the new compensation program was critical to the success of such a project. They believed that the best way to ensure staff acceptance was to involve them as much as possible. From an employee's point of view, any project that involves close examination of the employee's job or pay is threatening. Secrecy, real or perceived, would wreak havoc on morale. Or as Robert Townsend (1984) declares in *Further Up the Organization:* "Secrecy implies either: 1. 'What I'm doing is so horrible I don't dare tell you.' or 2. 'I don't trust you (anymore)' " (p. 201).

JOB ANALYSIS

The first step of the project was to look at the work performed by every employee. There are a variety of methods used to evaluate work performance of employees, usually involving some combination of the following: work logs maintained by the employee, descriptions of the employee's work by the immediate supervisor, observation of the employee's work, and questionnaires.

In the Downers Grove project, each employee kept a log of his/her work and used it to complete an inventory of the tasks performed. In completing the inventory, the employee was asked to indicate the percentage of work time devoted to each activity. Any activity that required work time less than 5 percent was listed in a separate section titled "additional duties." In this way the major components of each employee's job were isolated. Each employee also described the skills, knowledge, and training believed to be required in order to perform the job.

Each supervisor then examined his/her employees' job inventories and made additions or comments if needed. The supervisor did not change or remove anything that an employee had written, but only made comments as to whether the supervisor agreed with the employee's description or not. It was at this point that the department heads had the opportunity to consider the work of their departments as a whole and to determine whether positions needed to be restructured or redefined.

It was the administrative team's job to group "like" job inventories together and to write the job descriptions. The job description defined each position and would apply to all employees working in that position. Employees considered to be in the same position were those who performed the same primary tasks for about the same percentage of their work time.

In addition to a list of the duties of each position, a job description included the requirements for that position. At this time the administrative team took a close look at the skills, experience, and educational requirements for each position. The final form of each job description included the primary responsibilities (requiring 10 percent or more of the work time) and approximate percentage of work time spent on each, other duties (those requiring less than 10 percent of the time), the skills and experience required of employees in that position, and a statement concerning the training a new employee in that position would be given.

The final version of the job descriptions for most nonprofessional positions did not include an education requirement. The administrators agreed that, based on the library's actual hiring practices and general satisfaction with the result of those practices, specific job skills and experience should be the determining factors in filling positions. The job descriptions developed in the compensation project became the basis of the performance appraisal tool and also served as the primary tool used for advertising positions and recruiting staff.

In grouping similar descriptions, the administration obviously had some preconceived ideas of employees whose jobs were similar, but there were some surprises. A good example was the old position of clerk that became four distinctly different clerk positions: clerk, interlibrary loan clerk, circulation clerk, and data entry clerk. The clerk performed general clerical functions such as typing and filing. An interlibrary loan clerk was not only responsible for specific computer functions and other duties uniquely related to interlibrary loan work, but, through contacts with other libraries and the public, could have special impact on the image of the library. The data entry clerks have specific technical responsibilities as well as unique responsibilities involved in maintaining the card catalog and shelflist. The considerable amount of public contact and the concomitant impact on public relations distinguishes the job of circulation clerk from that of other clerks. After examining the job inventories of all the staff in these positions, the administrators agreed that the work and skills required of staff members in any one of these positions were different enough from that of any of the other clerk positions to merit a separate job description.

The first version of each job description produced by the administrative team was far from the finished project. The completed job descriptions were returned to the department heads for comment and evaluation. Whenever a job description applied to staff in more than one department, the department heads worked together to create a description that accurately applied to all the relevant employees. Once the department heads were satisfied with a description, it was passed on to the employees in that position for more comments. Any changes in the structure of a particular position were discussed by the department head and staff along with the new job description. Each description was discussed and revised several times at all levels before everyone was generally satisfied with the descriptions.

JOB RANKING

The grouping of the seventy-five individual job inventories resulted in twenty-five different job descriptions (for unique positions such as library director, artist, and custodian the description applied to only one person. Most job descriptions applied to a number of employees—e.g., there were nine circulation clerks and thirteen shelvers). These positions had to be evaluated to determine each position's worth or level of difficulty in relation to every other position. Three possible methods were considered for the project: whole job ranking, a classification system, and a point system.

In whole job ranking, a team of evaluators ranks each position against all the others. No system of measurement is used. The evaluators simply compare two jobs and judge which is more difficult. This method is simple and fairly quick to use. Proponents believe whole job ranking is fair because it is easier to compare two jobs and decide which is more difficult than to measure the absolute difficulty of one job. On the other hand, evaluators tend to look at the major elements of each job and ignore the minor components. The whole job ranking method is used to determine which of two jobs is more difficult, but the system includes no mechanism for determining how much more difficult it is. Also, it is hard to justify to employees because it is a judgment made by individuals with no explanation as to why or how the decision on a particular job was reached.

A classification system compares positions against predetermined descriptions of categories and slots each job into the category that best describes that job. Factors that might be considered in a classification's descriptions are education or qualifications required to perform the work, kinds of work performed, and responsibility. The same pros and cons apply to this as to ranking. It is relatively simple and quick to use, but this system also does not judge the overall worth of each job, and it can be difficult to explain why each position is ranked where it is.

The system chosen by the administrative team for the Downers Grove project was a point system. In this method a series of factors is selected and each factor has a number of levels (see figure 1). Every job is measured against each factor and awarded points depending upon which level of the factor most closely applies to the position. Figure 2 shows one of the factors used by Downers Grove—Responsibility/Accountability. A job description that was best described by level 3 of this factor would receive 180 points. The number of points earned from each factor is added, giving a score for the job. This total score provides a measure of the overall difficulty of the job.

Problems with this system include the difficulty in selecting the relevant factors for measuring the positions and defining the different levels of each factor. However, the point system was chosen because it would determine an absolute score (or level of difficulty) for each job, providing a way to compare positions performing different kinds of work. Also, the factors provided a clear method of explaining why a position was ranked the way it was, an important consideration in helping to ensure the acceptance of the project by the staff.

FACTORS

The most difficult aspect of the project was the creation of the

Factor	Weight	Points
Responsibility/Accountability	30%	300
Complexity of Job	30%	300
Contact with Others	15%	150
Supervision of Others	15%	150
Working Conditions	10%	100
Total	100	1,000

Figure 1. Job evaluation factors

This factor indicates the impact that an employee's error may have on the organization. The error may be in judgment or in processing activities related to job assignments. The error may have financial or human impact, result in loss of materials or data, or cause damage to equipment or facilities.

Points	Level	Description of Characteristics
0	0	Error in routine work results in minor inconvenience but has no impact which is obvious to the public.
60	1	Error in routine work will result in inconvenience to coworkers and may cause passing annoyance to the public.
120	2	Technical errors could impair services in this and other libraries or in other agencies in the community.
180	3	Error in work is generally confined in impact to a single public service department, and generally causes sharp criticism by the offended patron.
240	4	Technical or management errors may result in serious misdirection of departmental resources and staff. May cause major disruption in the library or in outside agencies.
300	5	Errors in planning or management may have serious impact on library resources and staff. Error likely to affect all departments. Serious error likely to affect public's perception of the library and affect their resulting level of support.

Figure 2. Responsibility/accountability

factors to be used to rank the job descriptions. The main reason the library administration decided to do the project in-house was to maintain the ability to adapt the project to the Downers Grove Public Library's priorities, hence the selection of factors to be used was critical.

Typical factors that an organization might use to evaluate a job include: responsibility/accountability, supervision exercised, contacts with others, confidentiality, complexity or problem-solving, working conditions, physical effort, and preparation and training (Beatty & Schneier, 1981, p. 479). In considering the possible factors, it was decided that not all were relevant to this organization. The selection of factors for this project was based on the administrator's desire to adapt the process to specific needs of the Downers Grove Public Library.

For example, working conditions and physical effort are factors that would be important when comparing jobs with work that is very different, such as janitorial work with that of clerks. Staff working in bookmobiles are often uncomfortable during extremes of weather, and this must be considered when comparing their work with that of other employees. But maintenance service for Downers Grove was contracted out to a cleaning company, and there were no branches or bookmobiles, and everyone worked in the same building. Given these circumstances, it was decided that separate factors for working conditions and physical effort were not necessary. Instead, one factor (titled working conditions) was created including elements of both. This factor considered elements such as the amount of time an employee might spend standing, using a CRT, or lifting and carrying things.

A separate factor for confidentiality was not found to be necessary. Basic tenets such as confidentiality of patron records apply to everyone on the staff, and nearly everyone has equal training in and access to the computer system containing registration and circulation records. Within the library's philosophy and written policy, there did not seem to be room for any gradations in this factor.

Ultimately five factors were identified for evaluating the twenty-five staff positions: responsibility/accountability, complexity of job, contact with others, supervision of others, and working conditions.

The value of having the library do this project in-house was most apparent in the development of the various levels of each factor and in the *weighting* of each factor. Figure 1 shows the number of points assigned to each factor.

A position rated at the highest level of every factor would receive a total of 1,000 points. The allocation of points between the factors indicates the weight (or relative importance to the organization) given to each factor. Responsibility/accountability, considered very important, increases 60 points each level for a maximum of 300 points for the highest level. Working conditions, given far less emphasis, increases 20 points each level to a maximum of 100 points for the highest level.

Figure 2 shows the levels of responsibility/accountability, with the number of points for each level. A position rated at level 1 would have a fairly low level of impact. Shelvers and most clerical positions were ranked at this level. Many technical positions, such as data entry clerk or interlibrary loan coordinator, were ranked at level 2. Level 3, in the middle, applied to positions with a high degree of public contact. This score was given to both reference librarians and circulation clerks. The department heads and the administrative secretary were ranked at level 4, while the library director and assistant librarian were ranked at level 5.

The factors were tested by having groups of staff use the factors to rate the new job descriptions. Each employee in a test group was given the descriptions of the factors, a stack of job descriptions, and a score sheet for each description. The employee read a job description, decided which level of each factor best applied to that description, and wrote the level and score on the score sheet.

In the first tests, the staff raters' scores for many of the positions varied enormously. After each round of testing, job descriptions and factors were examined to determine where problems existed. Job descriptions were reworked and clarified, and the descriptions of levels of some factors also had to be refined to better recognize the differences between positions. The arbitrary standard selected by the administrative team required that at least two -thirds of the ratings of a position had to agree on one level of each factor. In cases where this standard was not met, the job description was reworked and the position retested.

It is possible that a professional consultant would have been able to write clearer job descriptions and factors in less time. But the involvement of the staff in the testing process contributed to the staff's awareness of the project, hence there was no waste of time in revising and testing the project.

One serious problem with the design of the factors was discovered during the tests. As the library puts great emphasis on public relations, the factor of contact with others was originally weighted very heavily. In the first tests it was discovered that every position with any public contact at all received a total ranking far higher than positions which were far more complicated but which involved less public contact.

In reexamining the factors, it was obvious that elements of public contact were already covered in complexity of job and, to some degree, in responsibility/accountability. Therefore, the weight of the factor "contact with others" had to be reduced considerably with the points redistributed to responsibility and complexity.

The final rating of factors and job descriptions was done entirely by the library staff members. Rating sessions were scheduled in two-hour shifts and all interested staff members' work schedules were arranged to allow them to participate. The administrative team instructed the staff in the rating procedure and tabulated the results but did not take part in actually rating any position. Every job description, from shelver to library director, was included and each was rated by at least eighteen employees. In most cases nearly all raters scored a position at the same level of each factor with a few scores in the next higher or lower level.

At the time of the ranking, none of the job descriptions had been given titles. The descriptions were identified only by a letter code. During the ranking sessions, individual staff members often did not realize they had reached the job description of their own position until they were halfway through it.

DEVELOPING THE SALARY SCHEDULE

The next step in the project was to group positions that had received similar scores. This step demonstrated the usefulness of a point system. By providing a score, or absolute value, for each position, the system allowed the comparison of apples and oranges or shelvers and reference librarians. For example, the positions of data entry clerk (which received high scores for complexity and responsibility) and circulation clerk (with high public contact) were rated higher than other clerk positions, eventually becoming grade 4 positions. The other clerk positions received lower scores and became grade 3 positions.

The project resulted in sixteen distinct groups, and these groups became pay grades (see figure 3). The difference between pay grades was about 40 rating points.

There were some other interesting results. Because of the traditional bias toward the importance of reference work in libraries, the library assistants in the reference department had always been paid more

Grade	Job Title	Hourly Min. - Max	Annually Min. - Max.
1	Shelver I	$3.35 - 3.85	-
2	Shelver II Audio-Visual Aide Periodical Aide Processing Aide Custodial Aide	3.70 - 4.63	-
3	Clerk	4.00 - 5.20	-
4	Circulation Clerk Data Entry Clerk Custodian	4.50 - 6.08	-
5	Inter-library Loan Coordinator Cataloging Assistant Library Monitor	5.10 - 7.04	$9,945-13,728
6	Library Assistant	5.45 - 7.52	10,628-14,664
7	Circulation Supervisor Library Associate	5.95 - 8.21	11,603-16,010
8	Administrative Secretary	6.30 - 8.69	12,285-16,946
9	Library Program Coordinator Graphics and Display Coordinator	7.45 - 10.28	14,528-20,046
10	Librarian (part-time) Librarian (full-time)	9.27 - 11.59 9.27 - 13.60	18,077-22,601 18,077-26,520
11	Circulation Services Manager	9.60 - 13.63	18,720-26,579
12	Technical Services Manager	10.38 - 14.74	20,241-28,743
13	Literature & AV Services Coordinator Childrens' Services Coordinator	11.00 - 15.62	21,450-30,459
14	Reference & Information Coordinator	11.55 - 16.42	22,523-32,019
15	Assistant Librarian	13.00 - 18.85	25,350-36,758
16	Library Director	17.95 - 26.03	35,004-50,759

Figure 3. Employment classification and salary schedule for Downers Grove Public Library

than the library assistants in the literature department or children's department. In fact, the library assistants in the last two departments performed at least as much professional-level work, with less direct supervision, than the reference library assistants. The rating scores of these positions placed all three of the library assistant positions at about the same level or pay grade, ultimately giving the library assistants in the children's and literature departments a significant pay increase.

In another change, high points for supervision put the library assistants in the circulation department (who are regularly scheduled to be in charge of their department) on a higher grade than other library assistants, and this position's title was changed to circulation supervisor.

It was reassuring to the administrative team to observe that, while interesting differences between some jobs surfaced during the ratings, similar jobs generally did receive similar scores. The job descriptions for children's librarian and adult service librarian received the same score, for example. These positions are essentially equivalent; however the job description for children's librarian contained a much greater emphasis on programming, while the job description for adult services librarian emphasized patron assistance.

DETERMINING PAY

After the ranking process determined that job classifications fell into sixteen distinct levels, appropriate salaries had to be assigned to each. The method used by Downers Grove was a usage survey, the most common method for determining salaries. This requires selection of benchmark positions and surveying the job market to discover what comparable organizations pay for the same work.

The benchmark positions used for comparison were: clerk (grade 3), library assistant (grade 6), librarian (grade 10), and library director (grade 16). These positions are found in nearly every public library and employees in these positions generally have similar responsibilities in any library. The duties of individuals in many of the other positions would be likely to vary considerably from library to library and could not be used so easily for comparison.

Northern Illinois is fortunate to have the LACONI (Library Administrators Conference of Northern Illinois) salary survey. This is an annual survey of the salaries paid by public libraries and library systems. The survey includes minimum, maximum, and highest salary actually paid for each position surveyed. This survey was used to determine which libraries would be used for comparison of salaries of the benchmark positions.

In considering the makeup of the Downers Grove Public Library staff, it was known that almost all of the nonprofessional positions were part-time, from twelve to thirty hours per week. As is the nature of most part-time jobs, candidates for these positions came almost exclusively from the immediate vicinity. Therefore, the salaries of most interest to the purposes of the survey were those paid to clerks and library assistants by libraries located fairly close to Downers Grove.

On the other hand, most of the professional positions were full-time and the library wanted to attract qualified applicants from beyond the immediate area. The salaries of all the larger libraries in the survey were considered. As many of the larger and better paying libraries in Illinois were located in the Chicago suburbs, Downers Grove was, in effect, considering the salaries of the highest paying libraries in the entire state.

After the specific libraries to be studied were identified from the salary survey, each library was then contacted to verify that the actual work performed was close to that of the same position at Downers Grove and to verify the current salary paid by each library.

The board of trustees had determined, at the beginning of the project, that their goal was to offer salaries that were competitive with those of other libraries of similar size in the Chicago suburbs. Any organization planning a new compensation program has to make the decision of how competitive they want to be with the market. The decision could just as easily have been made to offer average salaries or even below average salaries. A survey of the market simply provides the information on which to base that decision. At any rate, once the pay range (minimum and maximum pay) of each benchmark position has been determined, the other grades are balanced in between.

Pay Ranges
One of the goals of the project was to develop a salary range with a minimum and maximum pay for each grade. In planning salary systems, pay ranges generally vary with a more narrow range for lower level positions and broader ranges for higher level positions. This reflects the investment in training time, the difficulty or complexity of the work, and degree of difficulty in replacing an employee at that position if he/she leaves. Increases from the minimum to the maximum of each range are often in equal steps.

The Federal Civil Service General Schedule is a typical example of a step salary schedule (see figure 4) (Krannich & Krannich, 1986, p. 237). The two lowest ranges, GS-1 and GS-2, have slightly narrower ranges of 25 percent from minimum to maximum pay. Each of the other ranges increases about 30 percent from minimum to maximum pay. Each step on any range is the same amount of money as every other step of that range. For example, each step of GS-3 is an increase of $382.

In a step system, raises are generally received annually (or on some other regular basis) as long as the employee's work is satisfactory. This is easy to administer and does not require any particular effort to be made to evaluate employees. A step system like this is very common in organizations that have developed a formal compensation system.

THE GENERAL SCHEDULE
Effective through 1986

	1	2	3	4	5	6	7	8	9	10
GS-1	$ 9,339	$ 9,650	$ 9,961	$10,271	$10,582	$10,764	$11,071	$11,380	$11,393	$11,686
2	10,501	10,750	11,097	11,393	11,521	11,860	12,199	12,538	12,877	13,216
3	11,458	11,840	12,222	12,604	12,986	13,368	13,750	14,132	14,514	14,896
4	12,862	13,291	13,720	14,149	14,578	15,007	15,436	15,865	16,294	16,723
5	14,390	14,870	15,350	15,830	16,310	16,790	17,270	17,750	18,230	18,710
6	16,040	16,575	17,110	17,645	18,180	18,715	19,250	19,785	20,320	20,855
7	17,824	18,418	19,012	19,606	20,200	20,794	21,388	21,982	22,576	23,170
8	19,740	20,398	21,056	21,714	22,372	23,030	23,688	24,346	25,004	25,662
9	21,804	22,531	23,258	23,985	24,712	25,439	26,166	26,893	27,620	28,347
10	24,011	24,811	25,611	26,411	27,211	28,011	28,811	29,611	30,411	31,211
11	26,381	27,260	28,139	29,018	29,897	30,776	31,655	32,534	33,413	34,292
12	31,619	32,673	33,727	34,781	35,835	36,889	37,943	38,997	40,051	41,105
13	37,599	38,852	40,105	41,358	42,611	43,864	45,117	46,370	47,623	48,876
14	44,430	45,911	47,392	48,873	50,354	51,835	53,316	54,797	56,278	57,759
15	52,262	54,004	55,746	57,488	59,230	60,972	62,714	64,456	66,198	67,940
16	61,296	63,339	65,382	67,425	69,468*	71,511*	73,554*	75,597*	77,640	
17	71,804*	74,197*	76,590*	78,983*	81,376*					
18	84,157*									

*The rate of basic pay payable to employees at these rates is limited to the rate payable for level V of the Executive Schedule, which would be $68,700.

Figure 4. The general schedule (effective through 1986)

Downers Grove chose not to use steps but instead to establish a range with a minimum and maximum pay for each position with raises geared to a merit pay system. An employee's percentage increase would be based on his/her annual performance evaluation. This would allow the library to meet the goal of rewarding good performance of employees.

To implement the new system, each current employee had to be placed somewhere within the pay range of their new pay grade. Although it would be convenient to place every employee at the bottom of the pay range for their position's grade, particularly in positions where the minimum pay was being increased considerably, such a move would be neither popular with the staff nor fair. Placing employees on the new salary range for their positions required considering each person's length of service, job performance, and current pay. One of the promises made to staff at the beginning of the project was that no employee would lose pay. Staff were warned that some employees might end up at the top of their salary ranges, but no one's pay would decrease.

In general, employees who had been in their present position for three to four years and whose performance was good were placed at about the midpoint of their salary range. Newer staff, who were not yet expected to be up to full speed, were placed about a quarter of the way up the range to place them ahead of new hires. The more experienced employees with longer service were placed proportionally (by length of service) throughout the top half of the range.

Because one of the library's goals was to be competitive with the market, the starting pay of nearly every position was raised, giving every employee, even new employees, an increase in pay. Professional salaries were particularly low, so librarians received about a 12 percent increase in salary the first year. The library assistants in the literature and childrens' departments, who had been paid significantly less than those in the reference department, received a considerable increase to bring them on par with others. The reference department's library assistant, relatively highly paid already, received only a small increase. Many other positions received sizable raises, bringing their salaries up to a competitive level.

Problems and Appeals

Initially, there were problems with several employees who had held their positions at the library for many years and who were already paid more than the maximum for their grade. These employees were frozen at their current pay until the salary schedule was adjusted upward enough to catch up. The library director had met, individually, with each of these employees to explain the situation.

At the time the new salary schedule was released to the staff, there was a review period. Any employee who felt that his/her position had been unfairly rated could appeal the rating. The first step in the process was to meet with the assistant librarian. At that point the employee and assistant librarian would review the job description and the factors used to rate the position, and discuss how the rating had been determined. If the employee still believed he/she had been unfairly treated, a staff committee would again rate the job description.

During the review period, two employees met with the assistant librarian to discuss the rating of their positions. One employee simply wanted the process explained again. The other case was more complicated. The question was not with the ranking of the employee's position but with the fact that the employee was often asked to help out in another service area when the department was shorthanded. The position that she was helping out in was ranked and paid at a higher grade than the employee's regular position. This was resolved by cautioning supervisiors that, barring emergency situations, staff should not generally be required to perform the duties of a higher pay grade. While this episode brought to mind horror stories of union shops that require six different employees to change a light bulb, the complaint was legitimate and the resolution fair. An employee should not be required to regularly perform tasks for which he/she is not paid. On May 1, the beginning of the next fiscal year, the new salaries went into effect.

The End of the Project?

The compensation program is ongoing. Policies needed to be developed to maintain the system. Every year the board examines the salary schedule in order to determine if changes to the overall schedule are needed, based on current surveys of the job market, to discover changes in the salaries paid the benchmark positions.

This evaluation of the salary schedule is done as part of the budget planning process and is separate from the performance appraisal process, although increases made to the salary system overall obviously reduce the amount of money available for merit increases. This evaluation and change in the overall system keeps the salary schedule viable and enables the library to continue to meet its goal of offering competitive salaries. This overall change in the schedule will also allow the maximum pay for any particular grade to eventually catch up with the veteran employees whose salaries were frozen by the limits of their grade's pay range.

In early 1987, as performance appraisals for the first increase based on the merit system were being completed, the salaries of several employees were still above the maximum for their grade. These employees were looking at the second round of raises for the rest of the library staff with no increase possible for them. The board of trustees was concerned that these veteran employees were being unfairly treated. The problem of "the top step" is universal, occurring wherever there is a maximum salary for a position. The problem has been discussed over and over, but no solution has yet been discovered that is completely satisfactory.

On February 24, 1987, the Downers Grove Board of Trustees approved a policy change that allows an employee whose salary has been frozen at the top of a pay grade for one year 50 percent of the raise that the employee's annual performance appraisal score would otherwise have earned. The administration believed that this policy was workable, particularly in consideration of the nature of the community. A large part of the potential job market for the library is made up of spouses of business and technical professionals employed in the area. This population is highly transient, reducing the possibility of accumulating a large number of staff earning wages far above the top of their salary ranges (according to the Annual Citizen Survey of the village of Downers Grove taken in August 1987, 25.5 percent of the population surveyed have been residents for five or fewer years and 42.9 percent have been residents for ten or fewer years). The board believed the risks of adopting this policy were worth taking to offset the negative effects on staff morale of not giving raises to these employees.

To ensure that the individual job descriptions remain viable, whenever an employee leaves the library the job description for that employee's position is examined by the assistant librarian and the department head. Is it still accurate? Does the description still fit all of the other employees who hold the position? If the job has changed significantly (and they do) what should be done? In most cases a change in the job description is adequate but not always.

To avoid straining the budget, positions are not upgraded easily. However, job descriptions with major changes are rated to make sure they still belong to the same pay schedule. If not, either job duties are reassigned appropriately or the position upgraded.

The updated job descriptions are used to advertise and hire the replacements for the positions. This avoids the trap of hiring new people who are qualified for the old job and then discovering that the job has changed over time.

Whenever a department proposes a new service, the proposal must include the job description for the staff who will be performing the work. If it is a responsibility added to an existing position, that job description must be reworked to include the new responsibility. The new job description must be rated to determine if the place of the position on the pay schedule should change. If the service requires the creation of a new position, a new job description must be created and then rated to see where it falls in the pay scale.

The administrators really believed the project was a success when several new staff positions were proposed and new job descriptions were created and rated. The ratings placed the positions on the salary schedule at levels that appeared reasonable both in comparison with the other positions in the library and in looking at comparable positions in the market.

COMMENTS

There are several reasons the Downers Grove project worked so smoothly. First, it was probably easier to start almost from scratch and build a new system than to try and restructure an existing system. There was almost nothing that wouldn't have been an improvement.

Second, the commitment from the beginning of the project to involve the employees, meant that it was their project too. It is likely that the main reason that there were so few requests for reconsideration of a position's ranking was because the staff helped write the job descriptions and did the ranking themselves. That this project was a library project resulted in a smooth transition and a successful project.

REFERENCES

Beatty, R. W., & Schneier, C. E. (1981). *Personnel administration: An experiential/skill-building approach* (2nd ed.). Reading, MA: Addison-Wesley Publishing Company.
Drucker, P. F. (1954). *The practice of management.* New York, NY: Harper & Row.
Krannich, R. L., & Krannich, C. R. (1986). *The complete guide to public employment.* Manassas, VA: Impact Publications.
Sibson, R. E. (1981). *Compensation.* New York, NY: Amacom.
Townsend, R. (1984). *Further up in the organization.* New York, NY: Alfred A. Knopf.
Wheeler, J. L., & Goldhor, H. (1981). *Wheeler and Goldhor's practical administration of public libraries* (revised by Carlton & Rochell). New York, NY: Harper & Row, pp. 88-89.

PEGGY SULLIVAN

Dean
College of Professional Studies
Northern Illinois University
DeKalb, Illinois

Allerton Park as Metaphor

ABSTRACT
Allerton Park Institutes are part of a long tradition, but the one in 1987
has been presented in a somewhat different way from earlier ones. There
were options on programs to attend, opportunities for considerable
interaction, a spirit of informality, and time to share problems and learn
from the problems of other participants. The setting of Allerton Park is
a metaphor for the activity. It has allowed for freedom and diversity,
humor and sociability, isolation and thought. It is a good place for a
group to gather, to get a better grip on its pride and purpose. It is
important for those of us who are administrators and leaders in librarianship to do this periodically, and we have benefited from this
experience.

THE ALLERTON EXPERIENCE

To appreciate the experience of this Allerton Park Institute, I
suggest a little context and a little nostalgia. I first attended an Allerton
Park Institute almost a quarter of a century ago, and it seemed to me that
all the giants of at least one field of librarianship were gathered there. I
have come back several times and have had that feeling each time. The
format would be a series of lectures, all delivered in this same room
designed as a library. It used to seem to me, as I looked across the rows of
listeners, that the sun streaming through those full-length windows
created haloes around their heads. They listened, and one or two might
have been asked in advance to comment on the papers presented. These
exchanges might turn into witty, even sharp, arguments, but the institute proceeded in a linear way, all of us experiencing the same stimuli,

discussing over good meals the same ideas, and coming to a point of culmination with the same content ringing in our heads and noted on our tablets, to be codified into proceedings at some point in the future.

This institute has not been like that. Presentations have been mixed, and we have been allowed to choose among several offered simultaneously. We have come primarily from academic and public libraries, and we have met in workshop settings where we have worked out problems and played roles as collective bargaining negotiators. We have not moved on the same emotional or intellectual lines so we have not had the sense of leading or being led, in some linear way, to some "group high" at the end of the institute.

The agendas we brought with us, rather than what was presented in any given session, have tended to occupy our conversations. This may have something to do with who we are. Like other Allerton Park conferees, we are a self-selected group of people who have been attracted by the topic. Women outnumber men among us by about two to one, which is low for the profession as a whole, but high for the administrative-leadership part of librarianship. More of us are public librarians rather than academic librarians, but in size and kind of libraries—private colleges, universities, district libraries, state agencies, suburban, metropolitan—we are broadly diverse. One-third of us are from Illinois, and I like that since it marks one of the characteristics of the University of Illinois—its strong links and mutual support within this state. Twenty-five other states are represented, which points to the other strength of the university—its leadership—which is not just regional, but national and even international. So we are diverse, too.

This morning and yesterday, as I once again explored the grounds of this interesting place, I realized that Allerton Park is a metaphor for this institute. Some of us have chatted about this. Is there no front door to this impressive building where we meet, or are there two front doors? I think it is the latter, with one of them opening to the stream, and the other to the lawn. The problem, of course, is that neither is in use, and we find ourselves coming and going through a fairly unprepossessing entrance on another side of the building.

Some of this same feeling of disorientation is evident throughout the estate. The long lines of Fu dog sculptures would seem appropriate to lead toward some central point of interest, and those sculptures of cute little musicians grinning at each other in two long lines would seem more appropriately followed by some culminating statue, but there is only the hard dirt path leading one to the statue of the gorilla bearing a woman away. A gorilla bearing a woman away? In 1987 that may seem pretty objectionable to some, but I am consoled to note that the gorilla is clinging fiercely to a rock in his free hand as though he knows the battle is not yet won. There is ambiguity in some of these images and experiences of discovering Allerton Park, but if one stayed home and just looked at some of the ten-cent postcards (and ten-cent postcards are somewhat of an anomaly themselves in this day and age), one would not know what is real here. One of the postcards refers to the emerald turf in the sunken garden, but dry brown leaves and good dark central Illinois soil were there when I walked through it. Is it any wonder that this place lends itself to an institute experience which is more like a mosaic than a graphic print?

Our presentations and informal conversations have also been mosaics. Since many of us are experienced as personnel administrators, getting information from others and analyzing what they have to say and putting it into a context that is useful to us in the future are all skills we have developed. We have had good opportunity to exercise them here.

Diverse as some of our perspectives may be, many of our concerns are similar. We are confronted with questions about why anyone would wish to be a librarian today. It is a demanding profession, it requires academic credentials which take their toll in time and money, and it does not seem to reward proportionally those who make that investment. Here, I come up with some old answers. One reason to be a librarian is that it provides the opportunity for smart people to continue to be generalists and to utilize their broad knowledge. There are places in librarianship for minds that are playful and for minds that are literal, as well as for those that combine both characteristics.

One of the most interesting insights I gained here was about the value of heroes in the organization, as Martin Maehr has identified them. As he noted, having heroes was the first clue that an organization was a good one, and having them acknowledged by others was the second clue to the quality of the organization. Then came the question: Why was the person a hero? In the answers to that question, there is room for individual taste.

Librarianship is a profession that encourages heroes, and it is encouraged by them as well. It provides opportunity for people to serve others in very direct and precise ways. It also still allows people to have highly individual approaches to their work. One librarian with whom I worked in the early years of my career may not be the best example of a hero. But he will always be a hero to me for a number of reasons, one of which was that, when the branch library where he was the supervisor was renovated and decorated with wooden ducks in flight across one wall, he objected to them. When it appeared that the bureaucratic processes of the public library where we worked were not responsive to his objections, he threatened to bring in his rifle and to shoot them down. They came down.

We do not have enough heroes, but it is good that we have some. Perhaps more critical in today's social context, we do not have enough minorities. It seems to me that librarianship has at least concerned itself with questions about the recruitment and retention of minorities longer than many similar professions. The success of those efforts is hard to document and evaluate.

Our history in this regard has provided some mixed experiences. The several reasons for recruiting minorities have not always been clear. We have erred, I believe, in thinking that minorities should always be preferred as librarians in minority communities. I know that librarians who are committed to service can be effective, even though they are not themselves minorities. Meanwhile, like other professions, librarianship is recognizing that the minorities often so painfully recruited may be lured to higher-paying or higher-prestige positions where they will be more visible as tokens in the environment rather than as role models for other minorities. Some of the conversations about this, like some of the conversations occurring here, become cyclical, confused, and discouraging, but I think there is some reason for pride in librarianship's continuing concern in regard to recruitment of minorities, even though it has been somewhat less than successful.

Another concern that has been expressed here can be looked at in several different ways. All of us have probably commented, at some time, on the need for good quality service in libraries as well as good quality in the personnel recruited to provide that service. We do not always remember that the measures of quality of service may have become more complicated, that the nature of service may have changed.

Library specializations exist and thrive today which were not even envisioned at the time I entered librarianship more than thirty years ago. However, there are some problems associated with these advancements. We need to be concerned about the fact that librarians are not always as willing to extend themselves as they might have been when individual specializations were less prevalent or less recognized. I have an example: A few weeks ago, a librarian friend who is working in the People's Republic of China wrote to request my assistance in getting a 100-item bibliography in earth sciences and related areas. He said that if he had such a bibliography he could use it as a buying list for the university where he was serving as consultant. It seemed like a rather simple request, and I thought a university library might be able to assist me. The first one I called said that they had no one with an advanced degree in the earth sciences, and no one who could provide that kind of expertise. Using the *ALA Membership Directory* I then called or wrote to several persons whose committee assignments or divisional appointments and locations suggested they might have that kind of expertise. I especially asked that if they could not provide such a bibliography themselves, they would forward my request to someone who could. In every instance, they replied to me, sometimes suggesting someone to whom I might write but more often saying they simply couldn't do it, or would need several months to do so. What I finally did was to photocopy pages from a standard bibliography in the sciences and send it to the librarian who requested it. It seems to me that somewhere between my lack of knowledge and my work assignment which is not in a library and the extensive knowledge of a subject specialist and a collection in the millions, it should have been possible to find fairly readily someone who might know some of the basic titles that should be on such a bibliography and be willing to devote perhaps one hour to compiling the 100 items. It is certainly true that there are always conflicts between the orientations of the specialist and those of the generalist. I believe that it will be unfortunate for librarianship if we lose all of the strengths associated with the latter as we focus appropriately on some of the needs and benefits of specialization.

There is perhaps some irony in referring to specialization in regard to library personnel practices. Libraries, for the most part, have not finally decided what they want in regard to specializations in personnel. Do all personnel officers in libraries need to have library experience? Library academic credentials? Are these neutral factors in the selection of personnel specialists? Are they positives? Are they sometimes negatives? Libraries are not historically consistent in how they answer these questions, and it must be admitted that chance and geography and other factors often play strong roles in selection of personnel specialists in libraries. There are similar questions about other specializations which are becoming more common in libraries, but are not always possessed by librarians. I am not suggesting that there is a single right decision to make in these areas, but I do believe that some recognition of the value of other specializations is appropriate for a profession which has matured to the extent that librarianship has.

As I suggested earlier, Allerton Park as a place is a kind of metaphor. It allows for freedom and diversity, humor and sociability, isolation and thought. It is a good place for a goup to gather, to get a better grip on its pride and purpose. It seems to me that has happened here for personnel people in libraries. The openness of sharing problems and of learning from the problems of other participants has been a good experience. It is true that there is more to experience and more to explore, but no one can expect one institute or one place to offer all answers. When a place is a metaphor it should come with a sense of wonder. Metaphors suggest relationships and bridge gaps. In that spirit, I have prepared what some might call a test, but what I prefer to call "a culminating experience" for participants in this institute. It was distributed to those attending the summary session and is provided in the Appendix. There are a few answers which are flexible, but, since there was no text for this experience, I can only confirm that all of the answers were given some time during this institute. Enjoy!

Appendix

A Culminating Experience Questionnaire for Critical Issues in Library Personnel Management

1. A first step in the educating/training process. _____
2. Major reason for turnover in library positions. _____
3. _____ _____ x *WE* (Work Experience) = Results _____
4. They resist change less when they have opportunities for conference attendance, etc. _____
5. This sends a mixed message, at best, when given for the wrong reasons. _____
6. This alone does not improve the quality of working life and may sometimes damage it. _____
7. Heroes are the first clue to its quality. _____
8. Collective bargaining requires skill at this. _____
9. This library officer is concerned with morale, productivity, training, recruitment—you name it! _____
10. His statement on library education and personnel utilization is still relevant, but would benefit from some revision. _____
11. An area of concern between library education prorams and libraries. _____
12. Acquiring job _____ is a responsibility shared by an institution and its staff. _____

*Answers to a Culminating Experience**

1. awareness; 2. lack of job challenge; 3. learning experience; 4. employees; 5. recognition; 6. technology; 7. organization; 8. negotiation; 9. personnel; 10. Asheim; 11. reference letter; 12. knowledge.

*Note that the initial letters of the answers spell "Allerton Park"

About the Contributors

SHARON L. BAKER is now Assistant Professor at the School of Library and Information Science, University of Iowa, Iowa City. Dr. Baker has been an administrator for five years and teaches library administration. She has spoken on the topic of change at the Mid-Atlantic Chapter of the Medical Library Association.

CHRISTOPHER F. BOWEN is Assistant Library Director of the Downers Grove Public Library in Downers Grove, Illinois. Mr. Bowen has chaired the ALA Membership Promotion Committee of the Intellectual Freedom Roundtable; is a member of ALA's Audio-Visual Committee; and Director at Large for Librarians for Social Responsibility of the Illinois Library Association. He wrote "Beyond Shhh! Developing a Library Discipline Policy" for *Illinois Libraries* (vol. 70, 1988).

CHARLES A. BUNGE is currently a professor at the School of Library and Information Studies, University of Wisconsin—Madison. He has served as president of ALISE (1980-81), of the Wisconsin Library Association (1972-73), of ALA/RASD (1987-88), and is a member of ALA/COA. Professor Bunge is author of "Stress on the Job: Reports from Library Staff Members" published in *Library Journal* (vol. 112, Sept. 15, 1987).

LUCY R. COHEN is manager of Personnel and Payroll Services at the University of Michigan Library in Ann Arbor. She is a member of ALA, ACRL, and LAMA. Ms. Cohen is also a continuing education instructor and guest lecturer on performance evaluation, training, recruitment, and other personnel related topics.

FREDERICK DUDA was head librarian at *The New York City Tribune* and has served as a library consultant from 1986 to 1988. He has contributed the "Biography of Warren J. Haas" for the *ALA World Encyclopedia of Library and Information Services* in 1986. Mr. Duda's publishing credits include writing articles for and coediting *Library Personnel Administration* (Neal-Schuman, 1981).

KATHLEEN M. HEIM is Dean and Professor at the School of Library and Information Science, Louisiana State University in Baton Rouge. Dean Heim has chaired the ALA's Office for Personnel Resources Advisory Committee and is co-principal investigator for a 1989 national study titled *Occupational Entry*. She is also editor of the journal *Public Libraries*.

NORMAN HOLMAN is presently Deputy Director of the Cleveland Public Library in Cleveland, Ohio. Mr. Holman has an M.A. in Library Science from the University of Wisconsin. His article, "Forces for Change in the Future of Collective Bargaining in Public Libraries" will be published in the *Journal of Library Administration* (forthcoming).

ANNE GRODZINS LIPOW is currently Director for Library Instructional Services at the University of California, Berkeley. She is a frequent speaker and author of articles on online catalogs, user services, staff development, and organizational change. Articles include "Training for Change: Staff Development in a New Age" to be published in the Fall 1989 issue of the *Journal of Library Administration* and "Impact of Online Systems on Library Staff" in the October 1989 issue of *American Libraries*.

MARTIN L. MAEHR is Professor of Education and Psychology at the University of Michigan in Ann Arbor. Professor Maehr has conducted research on motivation and achievement in the United States and abroad. he has also served as department chair and associate dean. He has numerous book and article credits and is an editor for a research annual *Advances in Motivation and Achievement*. Professor Maehr is also a consultant on motivation and organizational effectiveness.

CHARLES MARTELL is the Dean and University Librarian at California State University in Sacramento. Dean Martell is a member and former chair of the ALA Committee on Research. His many publications include *The Client-Centered Academic Library: An Organizational Model* (Greenwood Press, 1983); "The Nature of Authority and Employee Participation in the Management of Academic Libraries" in *College & Research Libraries* (vol. 48, March 1987); and "QWL Strategies: People are the Castle, People are the Walls, People are the Moat" in *Journal of Academic Librarianship* (vol. 10, no. 6, 1985).

JAMES G. NEAL is presently Assistant Dean and Head of Reference and Instructional Services Division of the Pennsylvania State University Library, University Park, Pennsylvania. His extensive publishing credits include "Evaluating Automated Systems—The User Perspective" in *Automation Projects: The Evaluation Stage* (ALA, 1988); "Changing Personnel Patterns for Library Automation" published in *Advances in Library Automation and Networking* (vol. 3, 1988); as well as numerous other published and forthcoming works on personnel management, public and technical services, and user library support.

RICHARD RUBIN is Assistant Professor at the School of Library Science, Kent State University in Kent, Ohio. Mr. Rubin's publications include "Employee Turnover Among Full-Time Public Libraries" in *Library Quarterly* (vol. 59, January 1989, pp. 27-46) and *Human Resources Management in Libraries* (Neal-Schuman, forthcoming). He has published several bibliographies and his professional interests include library use studies, personnel management, and intellectual freedom in libraries. He has also participated in workshops and presented papers on various subjects of library science ranging from administrative matters to patron use and access.

PEGGY SULLIVAN is Dean of the College of Professional Studies at Northern Illinois University in DeKalb. Dean Sullivan is a frequent speaker at library conferences and is a contributor to the literature in the areas of children's literature, storytelling, library education, public library administration, school media center administration, etc.

INDEX

Academic libraries: compensation systems, 103-25; exit interviews, 34-36; merit systems, 117; salary surveys, 112

Anderson, A. J., 65-66

ALA. *See* American Library Association

ALA Survey of Librarian Salaries, 112

American Library Association, Office for Library Personnel Resources, 28, 116

ARL. *See* Association of Research Libraries

Association of Research Libraries (ARL), 112

Automation planning and employee participation, 58

Bell, Keith, 87

Bunge, Charles, 87

Burnout. *See* Stress

Byrd, Richard, 88-89

Change: effects of, 54-56; employee participation, 57-58; fear of, 54-56, 58-59; job performance, 57; library values, 60; negative employee behavior, 54-61; need for, 59; resistance to, 53-61, 63-65; resources commitment, 59-60; training, 62-70; work climate, 60-61

Civil Rights Act of 1964, 114-15

Clark, Ruth, 67

Cleveland Public Library, 14-15

Collective bargaining: dispute resolution procedures, 12-16; interest arbitration, 16-17; management rights, 17-20; public employees, 11-20

Compensation systems: developing, 103-25, 127-42; academic libraries, 103-26; administration of, 119-22; American Library Association, 116; comparable worth, 115-16; designing of, 109-13, 127-42; discrimination, 114-16; Downers Grove (Illinois) Public Library, 127-42; fringe benefits, 118-19; governmental influences on, 113-16; job analysis, 106-09, 130-31; job ranking, 107, 131-35; merit-based systems, 116-18, 120-21, 139-40; objectives of, 105-06, 128; salaries, 110-13, 135-41; unions, 116

"Corporate Leadership Skills: A New Synthesis," 88-89

Davis-Bacon Act, 113

Dayton Classroom Teachers Association *v.* Dayton Board of Education, 11-12

Discrimination. *See* Compensation systems

District 925, Service Employees International Union, 14-15

Downers Grove (Illinois) Public Library, 127-42

Drug testing, 19

Education, library, 22, 28-30

"8 Ways to Ruin Performance Review," 41-42

Employee commitment: 3-10; importance of, 4-5; encouragement of, 5-6; to training, 65-67

Employee satisfaction, 87

Employee turnover: causes of, 33, 37-38

Entry-level recruitment, 21-30

Equal Pay Act, 114-15, 117

Evaluation, performance. *See* Performance evaluation

Every Employee a Manager, 65-66

Exit interviews: 32-39; benefits and liabilities of, 37-39; and employee turnover, 33; evaluation, 38; format of, 35-36; post-turnover surveys, 36-38; sample questions for, 36; and use in libraries, 34

Factor comparison in job evaluations, 107-08

Fair Labor Standards Act (FLSA) 1988, 114

Federal Civil Service General Schedule, 138

Ferguson Act, 11